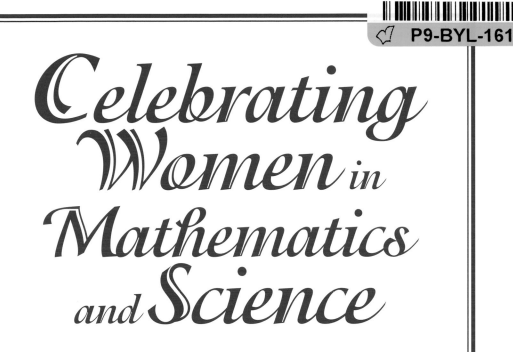

Celebrating Women in Mathematics and Science

Edited by

Miriam P. Cooney, csc
SAINT MARY'S COLLEGE
NOTRE DAME, INDIANA

NATIONAL COUNCIL OF TEACHERS OF MATHEMATICS
Reston, Virginia

Copyright © 1996 by
The National Council of Teachers of Mathematics, Inc.
1906 Association Drive, Reston, VA 22091-1593
All rights reserved

Library of Congress Cataloging-in-Publication Data:

Celebrating women in mathematics and science / edited by Miriam P.
Cooney.
    p.   cm.
    Includes bibliographical references.
    ISBN 0-87353-425-5 (pbk.)
    1. Women mathematicians—Biography—Juvenile literature.   2. Women
scientists—Biography—Juvenile literature.   I. Cooney, Miriam P.
QA27.5.C45   1996
509' .2'2—dc20   96-14119
                                                                      CIP
                                                                      AC

Printed in the United States of America

Dedication

This collection is lovingly dedicated by its authors to its young readers, the scientists and mathematicians of the future who observe and ask questions, guess and test their guesses, like to make things work, want to know how things work, love to solve problems, and ask why and why not. May they find inspiration in these tales of mathematicians and scientists who were once young readers like themselves.

Despite her reluctance, the authors also dedicate this book to Sister Miriam P. Cooney. Sister Miriam has been associated with Saint Mary's College, Notre Dame, Indiana, for more than fifty years as a student, as a faculty member, and as chair of the mathematics department. A recipient of Saint Mary's prestigious Spes Unica Award, she is recognized for her excellent teaching and dedicated service. Sister Miriam is also recognized nationally as an advocate for women in science and mathematics.

Throughout the year of her seminar entitled Mathematics, Science, and Gender, Sister Miriam inspired us and awakened in us a belief in our own abilities and a passion to reach out and inspire the young women in our charge. She taught us how to help them develop positive attitudes about mathematics and science and encouraged us to assume responsibility for the truism that we teachers can make a difference. Sister Miriam is a woman of rare quality, a superior educator, and an exemplary woman of mathematics.

Table of Contents

Preface

This collection of stories of great women in mathematics and science is the work of twenty classroom teachers of mathematics and science who took the opportunity to add a yearlong seminar to their busy days. Throughout the academic year 1991–92, these teachers studied literature and current research in issues related to mathematics, science, and gender. In their enthusiasm for discovering many great women, each volunteered to write the story of at least one woman, thus enabling their students to join them in celebrating these discoveries. The authors hope that middle school and junior high school girls and boys, for whom this volume is written, will discover the rich lives and work of many women throughout history who contributed significantly to the development of science and mathematics.

Kathleen Thomas, coordinator of the Writing Center at Saint Mary's College, assisted the teachers in preparing their contributions.

The publication of this book is the result of collaboration among members of the NCTM Headquarters editorial and design and production staffs. In particular, Debra Kushner was responsible for the design of the book and Sheila Gorg for editing the stories.

The cost of preparing the manuscript was borne by another woman of mathematics, Marie Hank McKellar, a Saint Mary's College graduate (1962). Now retired, she was a professor of mathematics for more than thirty years at Mercy College, Dobbs Ferry, New York. We thank her for her patronage in making this volume possible. A grant of Eisenhower Program funds for the seminar was provided by the Indiana Commission on Higher Education, for whose support we are grateful.

Miriam P. Cooney, csc
Saint Mary's College
Project Director

Hypatia

—Mathematician and Martyr for Truth

The time of the persecuted Christian had passed, and the Holy Roman Empire ruled most of the modern world. In the port city in Egypt known as Alexandria, Christians fought pagans for power. Into this turbulent world, I was born. I was named Hypatia, and the year was 370.

My father, Theon, was a professor at the University of Alexandria. He taught mathematics there and was later named director of the university. Father told people that he could create the perfect human. I was the subject of this experiment. This endeavor started out well except that I was born a girl. My father schooled me in art, literature, science, and philosophy. I loved to be at the museum, which is what we called the university. True to Greek tradition, I also learned to swim, row, ride horseback, and climb mountains. Because the Roman culture believed rhetoric was the most important pursuit, I was also trained in speech. As I grew, my father announced that I had surpassed his knowledge in mathematics, so he sent me to study in Athens.

After my studies in Athens, I traveled throughout Europe for about ten years. My beauty was proclaimed wherever I went. I was received by princes and philosophers of many countries, some of whom asked for my hand in marriage. I always told them that I was already married to the truth. My father had taught me to study everything and to take nothing at face value. I applied this philosophy to marriage as well as to religion. In the Greek culture of the time, a wife was to serve her husband and his guests, but she was not to enter into their conversations. A virtuous wife was to be beautiful and silent. I rejected the role of the submissive wife who must always defer to her husband.

My father also influenced my understanding of religion. He taught me to ask questions and to analyze everything. I could not accept dogmatic beliefs without first questioning them. Christianity required that I believe, on faith only, in a man who had died several hundred years earlier. Neoplatonism allowed me to question, gave me the freedom to grow, and permitted me to seek truth with an open mind. Therefore I refused to choose any religion or cult. In my day this refusal to choose determined my friends, my enemies, and even my death.

When I returned to Alexandria, I was invited to teach at the university. I taught geometry and astronomy there, but my favorite subject was the new mathematics of the day, algebra. When my students had a difficult time with an algebra book written by Diophantus, I wrote a commentary on the book and constructed new problems for this new concept in mathematics. I also wrote treatises on mathematics titled *Astronomic Canon of Diophantus* and *Conics of Apollonius*, and my father and I coauthored a commentary on Euclid's work. It is unfortunate that most of my books, as well as those of Sappho and many other important people of our time, were destroyed when the library of Alexandria was ransacked and burned. However, in the fifteenth century a few of my books were found in the Vatican library.

I had some wonderful students. Among them was Synesius of Cyrene, who later became the bishop of Ptolemaïs. He tried his best to protect me from the Christians. It was good of him to save my letters and to write so eloquently about me. We had wonderful discussions with many of my students and peers, often in my library. Nicephorus and Philostorgius called me a genius. My students considered me an oracle and called me the Muse. One of my dear friends was Orestes, who was also a Neoplatonist. He became the prefect of Egypt.

Over the years I was given time to develop some of my ideas into practical instruments. When at sea, sailors would die of thirst even though they were surrounded by water, so I developed a way to distill sea water. I understand that this process is still used today. I wrote instructions for constructing an astrolabe, a device that had been used for centuries to help sailors navigate. This instrument continued to be used to find the elevation of the stars until the sextant was invented. Because I also loved to work in astronomy, I designed a planisphere, a chart of the stars and their movements across the sky.

Although my life was good and I was given many opportunities usually reserved for the elite male population, trouble still came my way. It must have been around 412 that Cyril was named patriarch of Alexandria. The Neoplatonists had always had differences with the Christians. As Cyril's influence grew, his followers began to oppress us more brutally than any group had before. Synagogues were burned to the ground, and the growing struggle for political power caused ever deeper divisions between the Christians and others. The Christians blamed the Neoplatonists for every misfortune, and many non-Christians seemed only too happy to take part in a good fight.

My friend Orestes was not going to give up the prefect's position easily. The bishop, Cyrene, was worried about my safety and tried to protect me, but I told him that I would not let some power-hungry tyrant keep me from my students. Cyril (or one of his followers) spread a horrible story that if "the virgin" (which is what they called me) were sacrificed, the rulers could come to an agreement. He knew that eliminating me and my influence over my students would further weaken the prefect's power. Cyrene's concern for my safety increased; he begged me to stay in safe places. At the same time the Christians kept pressuring me to join them. Cyril would do anything to lessen my influence over my students.

I recall that fearful day in late 415. I was on my way to the university when an angry mob, rioting in the streets, slowed my chariot. Among the mob was Peter the Reader, who had a great deal of control over the Christians. Peter sincerely believed his calling was righteous, which made him all the more dangerous. Disturbances like this were common occurrences in those days. I thought everything would be all right if I stayed out of the way until I could pass and get inside to safety. Then suddenly, I was torn from my chariot by my hair and dragged through the streets to the mob's church. I knew that my days of being a pawn between those on Cyril's side and those on Orestes' side were over. The mob was huge and terrifying. They came at me with sharp oyster shells. They scraped away the flesh from my bones, tore my limbs from my body, then threw the pieces into a fire. Afterward, they stood chanting victoriously, as if my death marked a great date in history.

Historians claim that my death marked the end of the growth of mathematics in the Western world for approximately one thousand years. Religion became involved with the pursuit of power, and all other intellectual pursuits came under the scrutiny of the religion in power at the time. How sad that all learning, even mathematics, should suffer in such power struggles. Still, I rejoice in the knowledge that mathematics continues to grow in scope and influence.

Debra Fields Rogers
Jimtown High School
Elkhart, Indiana

Suggested Reading

Bergamini, David. *Mathematics*. Life Science Library. New York: Time, 1963.

Boyer, Carl B. *A History of Mathematics*. 2nd ed. New York: John Wiley & Sons, 1991.

Mozans, H. J. *Woman in Science*. Notre Dame, Ind.: University of Notre Dame Press, 1991.

Osen, Lynn M. *Women in Mathematics*. Cambridge: MIT Press, 1974.

Smith, David E. *History of Mathematics*. New York: Dover Publications, 1958.

Emilie du Châtelet

—"Venus-Newton"

Dances and fancy ball gowns or algebraic equations? Motherhood or Newton's laws of motion? Entertaining at a French château or serious research? Which would you choose?

Young Gabrielle-Emilie le Tonnelier de Breteuil decided not to limit herself by choosing one aspect of life over another. She managed to incorporate both social and intellectual worlds into her life with flair and success.

Emilie, born in France in 1706, became a scientist and mathematician. We are fortunate that in the eighteenth century, the custom of frequent letter writing was so much a part of the culture that even people in the same house wrote to one another. As a result, we now have interesting and accurate information available to us about Emilie du Châtelet and her life and times.

For example, we know that Emilie's father, Louis Nicholas le Tonnelier, the baron de Breteuil, said some unusual things about his daughter. He once described her in this way (Perl 1978, p. 30):

Were it not for the low opinion I hold of several bishops, I would prepare her for a religious life and let her hide in a convent. She stands as tall as a girl twice her years, she has prodigious strength, like that of a wood-cutter, and is clumsy beyond belief. Her feet are huge, but one forgets them the moment one notices her enormous hands. Her skin, alas, is as rough as a nutmeg grater, and altogether she is as ugly as a Gascon peasant recruit in the royal footguards.

Because Emilie's father was troubled about her clumsiness, he helped her develop her horseback-riding skills. And because he doubted that she would ever marry—considering her appearance—he also became interested in Emilie's education.

Very few women were educated at that time. The only opportunity for most girls to learn was in a convent school. Emilie's mother had had a convent-school education and tried to train her own children. Here are a few things that she felt were important to pass on:

1. Do not blow your nose on your napkin.
2. Break your bread and do not cut it.
3. Always smash an eggshell when you have eaten the egg.
4. Never comb your hair in church.

Emilie's mother's education was particularly concerned with manners. Why, then, did Emilie's education emphasize academics? There were three significant reasons. First, Emilie was fortunate enough to be born into an aristocratic family (her father was the head of protocol at court) that could afford to send her to school and to hire competent tutors. Second, Emilie proved to be very bright. At age twelve, she knew Italian and Latin and played the spinet. At fifteen, she translated books into French. Her many abilities qualified her to study advanced topics. The third reason is related to her father's opinion of her. Since Emilie's father was convinced that she would never marry, he was eager to hire the best tutors for her. He hoped that an outstanding education would help compensate for her life without a husband and family.

Over the years, Emilie turned out to be a superior equestrian and an outstanding scholar, and contrary to her father's expectations, Emilie married at the age of eighteen. She married an older man, but they seemed compatible at the time.

Emilie had wanted to marry a man who was in the same social class as her father. The thirty-three-year-old Marquis Florent Claude du Châtelet Lomont fit the bill. He held an even higher rank than Emilie's father, and although he did not have many cash assets, he owned several estates. Emilie believed that an older husband would be less likely to interfere with her personal life and would give her the freedom she needed to pursue her studies.

For his part, the marquis was delighted with Emilie. She was five feet, nine inches tall, which at that time was considered exceptionally tall for a woman—even for a man. Although she was somewhat homely, Emilie made herself attractive. She wore lace, perfume, and fine clothes, and she used makeup and jewelry to her advantage. The marquis wanted heirs to his estate, and he knew that Emilie was a strong, healthy young woman who would give him children. Fortunately, he was flattered to have an intelligent wife, so Emilie was able to continue her scholarly pursuits.

Emilie and the marquis had three children—one girl and two boys. Unfortunately, one of the sons died at an early age.

Emilie and her husband were frequently separated. The marquis had to leave for months at a time to be with his regiment. While he was away, Emilie spent much of her time at court, attending parties and gambling.

Although Emilie led a very active social life, she never neglected her studies—especially the study of mathematics. Emilie would not allow the prejudices of society to weaken her desire to learn and share her knowledge of mathematics and science. For example, when Emilie wanted to attend a certain café in France that was a gathering place for scientists and mathematicians, she was told that only men were allowed. She promptly went home, returned dressed as a man, and was admitted.

When she was twenty-six, Emilie became a close companion to a man who remained a dear and loyal friend until her death. He was a very famous writer named François Marie Arouet, better known as Voltaire. At one point in his life he was hailed as the greatest living French poet. In addition to his writing, Voltaire's interests included mathematics, business, and science. He worked in the export trade and was always interested in new business ventures. In 1729 he won a lottery. Voltaire had calculated that his winnings would be greater than his expenses if he bought all the tickets—so he did. As a result of his shrewdness, he was never short of cash. His wealth allowed him to make an unusual but interesting arrangement with Emilie.

Voltaire was about forty when his relationship with Emilie began. He was on the verge of arrest for some writing that had offended the monarch, Louis XV, so he rented space in one of the Marquis du Châtelet's estates, the château at Cirey. A château is a huge country home or castle located on a large parcel of land in the French countryside. These estates were grand and luxurious. The estate at Cirey was near the Belgian border and offered Voltaire a quick escape from the country if orders for his arrest were issued.

After Voltaire moved in, he decided to use his own money to make repairs and add an extra wing. Emilie and her children followed Voltaire to the château at Cirey and arrived with two hundred pieces of luggage. Emilie immediately took charge of the renovation and worked with Voltaire to create a unique arrangement. They had separate suites connected by a long hall. This hall was appointed with the latest in scientific equipment for experimentation and study.

Emilie and her children spent many years at the château. Her husband would come to visit occasionally. Emilie saw her children daily, but they were raised primarily by nurses and governesses, as was the custom of the time. For the most part, Emilie and Voltaire spent their days on their work in mathematics and science and their evenings on entertaining frequent guests. They had a theater built at the château and would see or act in plays with their guests. Longchamp, a servant at the château, wrote the following of Emilie (Osen 1974, p. 65):

> Mme du Châtelet passed the greater part of the morning with her writings, and did not like to be disturbed. When she stopped work, however, she did not seem to be the same woman. The serious air gave place to gaiety and she gave herself up with the greatest enthusiasm to the delights of society. She might have been taken for the most frivolous woman of the world.

Emilie produced some significant work during this period. When she was unable to find a suitable science textbook for her son, she decided to write her own. She wrote *Institutions de physique,* a book on the scientific method that included the work of Leibniz, one of the mathematicians often credited with the development of calculus.

When this work was published in 1740, one of her tutors, Samuel Koenig, claimed that it was a summary of the lessons he had designed for her. Emilie was outraged and set out to prove that he was lying. She appealed to Pierre de Maupertuis, one of her former tutors and a leading mathematician and astronomer. Maupertuis was a fellow of the English Royal Society and a member of the French Academy of Science. He had at one time been president of the Berlin Academy. He could confirm that the ideas in Emilie's book were indeed her own, because she had discussed some of them with him long before Samuel Koenig had tutored her. (After Emilie's death, letters were found that proved that Koenig had lied.) This episode was extremely difficult for Emilie. Most of her peers agreed that she was certainly capable of writing the book, but Emilie was convinced that Koenig's accusations were more readily accepted by the scientific community because she was a woman.

Emilie du Châtelet wrote only one nonscientific book: *Traités sur le bonheur,* a collection of writings on happiness and moral philosophy.

In 1738 the Academy of Science offered a prize for an essay on nature and the diffusion of fire. Each entrant had one year to complete and submit an essay. Voltaire entered the contest and devoted weeks to his research and writing. He and Emilie discussed the topic at length, and when she began to disagree with him, she decided to enter the contest herself under an assumed name. Emilie had only one month to write and submit her own entry. She worked unceasingly and secretly. Neither she nor Voltaire won first prize, but both papers were considered so good that they were published with the winning entry.

Emilie was usually very open about her abilities and her contributions to science. Therefore, scholars have speculated that she concealed her identity when entering the contest in deference to Voltaire.

Another of Emilie's endeavors during her time at the Château de Cirey was the study of the concept of scientific method. Sir Isaac Newton's ideas on the subject were new, and scientists were interested in its application to understanding not just physical forces but social forces as well. Her last work of this period was a paper on optics. Emilie would often function on just two to four hours of sleep when she was engaged in a project. Although she and Voltaire both lived at the château, houseguests said that except for meals, the two rarely saw each other when they were working.

After ten years together, Voltaire and Emilie decided to separate. She resumed the place at court she had left when she joined Voltaire at Cirey. She then was given the privilege of being among the select courtiers of the queen, Maria Leszczynska. Emilie enjoyed this life of parties, gambling, and the company of powerful men.

Emilie's personality had two different sides. On the one hand, she enjoyed the frivolous role of the partygoer—the fancy dresses, balls, gambling, and flirtations. On the other hand, she was a serious scientist who conducted complicated experiments and published important works. Emilie had a unique approach to this dual life. She knew what to expect from different people and what they expected from her. For example, she would never expect her tutors to admire her fancy gowns; instead, she realized that they would admire her ability to do nine-digit multiplications in her head. And she would not expect her friends in the salons of Paris to appreciate her research on physics; rather, she knew that they would value her ornate jewelry.

Gambling was a big part of Emilie's frivolous side. While gambling one evening in 1748, Emilie lost 84 000 francs. This episode prompted her to retreat from the Paris social life and try to find a way to pay her debts. Her loyal friend Voltaire went with her. They stayed in Lunéville in Lorraine as guests at the court of King Stanislaus. At this time Emilie became pregnant with her fourth child.

During the pregnancy, Emilie and Voltaire returned briefly to Cirey to work on finances. While there, Emily became concerned that she would not survive childbirth because of her age.

Voltaire and Emilie returned to Paris, where Emilie worked diligently on a French translation of *Principia mathematica*, Newton's famous work on the principles of mathematics. After finishing the translation, Emilie added her own commentary.

After five months in Paris, Voltaire took Emilie back to Lunéville to obtain proper medical attention. Emily continued her work until she gave birth to a little girl three months later. Unfortunately, Emilie's fears about surviving childbirth were not unfounded. Only a few days passed before both she and the baby died in 1749.

Emilie's translation of the *Principia* was published six years after her death. The ideas presented in this book were new and revolutionary. Emilie's French translation made an important contribution to the spread of Newton's scientific knowledge to a large portion of Europe.

To put Emilie's work in science and mathematics in perspective, we need to consider what other women of the day were accomplishing academically. It wasn't until the late seventeenth century (just shortly before Emilie was born) that the first state school for girls was established in France. Since only the daughters of the nobility could attend this school, most girls could not even read. The alternative to the state school was a convent school, where girls were sent at about five years of age. They returned in time to be married.

Not only was an education unavailable to most women, but those who were lucky enough to be students were ridiculed by society. Two plays that were very popular in France at the time demeaned educated women. Molière's comedies *Les précieuses ridicules* and *Les femmes savantes* portrayed education as undesirable for women. Most men at this time believed that women were incapable of serious scholarship.

Despite the prevalent attitudes, Emilie managed to excel in her pursuit of learning. She was respected by those in her field and even had students seek her out as a tutor. She called those who came to study with her at Cirey *Emiliens*. She contributed to science as an educator as well as a researcher and a writer.

H. J. Mozans, the author of *Woman in Science* (1991, p. 202), credits Emilie with being the first woman in more than a thousand years to discuss physics:

> All things considered, the Marquise du Châtelet deservedly takes high rank in the history of mathematical physics. In this department of science she has had few, if any, superiors among her own sex. And, when we recollect that she labored while the foundations of dynamics were still being laid, we shall more readily appreciate the difficulties she had to contend with and the distinct service which her researches and writings rendered to the cause of natural philosophy among her contemporaries.

Emilie has no living descendants. Her daughter married a duke but never had any children. Her son served as ambassador to London but died on the guillotine, and his only son lost his life during the revolution. Emilie's work and her example are her legacy.

This legacy includes not only her contributions to mathematics and science but also the influence of other aspects of her life on subsequent generations. It is easy to measure her scientific contributions by recounting her research and publications. Her influence on other young women to pursue their academic gifts is, however, more difficult to measure. Emilie's life and work certainly showed other eighteenth-century women that they did not need to choose between the seemingly opposite worlds of high society and higher education.

The two sides of Emilie—her zest for life and her zest for learning—were best summarized by King Frederick II of Prussia when he fittingly referred to her as "Venus-Newton."

Delphine Luzney
Saint Joseph's High School
South Bend, Indiana

Suggested Reading

Durant, Will, and Ariel Durant. *The Age of Voltaire*. New York: Simon & Schuster, 1965.

Mozans, H. J. *Woman in Science*. Notre Dame, Ind.: University of Notre Dame Press, 1991.

Osen, Lynn M. *Women in Mathematics*. Cambridge: MIT Press, 1974.

Perl, Teri H. *Math Equals: Biographies of Women Mathematicians + Related Activities*. Menlo Park, Calif.: Addison-Wesley Publishing Co., 1978.

Smith, David Eugene. *History of Mathematics*. New York: Dover Publications, 1951.

Maria Gaetana Agnesi

— A Passion for Mathematics and Health Care

At age five, Maria Gaetana Agnesi was a typical Milanese girl: dark eyed and dark haired, with a dark complexion. Less typical was her fluency in both French and her native Italian. Maria's intellectual abilities—in particular, her fantastic memory—were recognized early in her life. Maria grew up to become a renowned mathematician.

The first child of Pietro Agnesi and Anna Fortunato Brivio, Maria Gaetana was born 16 May 1718 in Milan, Italy. Her father, a cultured nobleman who had purchased a title, taught mathematics at the University of Bologna. Both her parents came from wealthy merchant families. This background afforded young Maria the opportunities of the upper class.

Eighteenth-century Italian women were often educated in convents, where life was rigorous. Their education usually began at age five and often continued until their family required them to enter into an arranged marriage. The curriculum was rudimentary, perhaps including reading and writing but certainly dressmaking and social skills. The recitation of the rosary was part of the discipline of the convent. As adults, these upper-class Italian women were put on a pedestal, like decorations to be admired.

Although most Italians of the time viewed the education of women as frivolous, it was not uncommon to find women who lectured and held positions as university professors. This was the age of the Enlightenment; tradition was often challenged by newer thinking based on reason. The women who received an education were likely to have been taught by the tutors employed to teach the male children of the family. A lower-class family could not afford to employ tutors; therefore, education for the girls of these families was unattainable.

Maria Gaetana's situation was unusual. Delighted with his young prodigy's exceptional abilities, Pietro Agnesi employed tutors specifically to train and encourage his daughter. The special relationship between fathers and daughters was particularly strong in Italian culture. Although Maria Gaetana and her father were close, Pietro Agnesi expected strict obedience. Maria was obedient, but she frequently challenged her father's demands.

Around the age of nine, Maria Gaetana received further training in Greek, Hebrew, Spanish, and other languages. Maria's talents were "exhibited" by her father in one of his famous academic meetings, often held in the evening at the Agnesi home. In Latin, Maria Gaetana recited Horace's discourse advocating higher education for women.

Latin was the language of scholars and scholarship. It gave people of learning throughout Europe a common means of communication. Pietro's academic evenings often continued to feature young Maria Gaetana, debating in Latin the various virtues of mathematics, science, and philosophy. (Almost two hundred of the theses she defended are found in her second work, *Propositiones philosophicae*, published in 1738.) Often Pietro's mood became lighter during these soirees. Following the Latin debates,

Maria Gaetana would converse with the guests in their native languages. She was truly a brilliant linguist!

Maria Gaetana's younger sister, Maria Teresa, was a gifted musician. She, too, was pressed into service during these academic evenings. Specially trained by tutors, Maria Teresa entertained the guests with original compositions performed on the harpsichord at "intermissions" throughout the evening. Pietro Agnesi and his evening salons soon became the talk of Milan.

These evenings continued until Maria Gaetana was twenty and begged her father's permission to retire to a convent. Her father refused her request; always obedient, Maria Gaetana honored his wishes. The doting father did, however, agree to three requests from his daughter: Maria Gaetana could simplify her dress, making it more modest; she could attend church as often as she liked; and she would not be forced to attend social events such as balls or the theater.

Maria Gaetana had always been an introvert and disliked being put on display. After her mother died in 1732 while giving birth to her eighth child, Maria Gaetana began a new occupation—managing the household and educating her younger brothers. She continued these responsibilities even after her father remarried twice and had had a total of twenty-one children. Maria Gaetana eventually became a housekeeper, at one time or another, to all twenty siblings.

During this time, Maria Gaetana spent more than a decade developing her mathematical abilities. She became so dedicated a scholar that mathematics consumed her. Maria Gaetana's intense concentration kept her awake until late at night, and many sleepless nights ended only when exhaustion overtook her. Maria Gaetana apparently once wrote out the solution to a difficult problem in her sleep. She discovered the solution, in her handwriting, on her desk the next morning. These early years of intense study affected her health, and her family doctor told her to exercise more frequently. Sometimes after physical exertion, however, she would have nerve seizures.

In 1748, Maria Gaetana's two-volume work, *Instituzioni analitiche*, or *Analytical Institutions*, was published. Calculus had been developed in the previous century, and information about it was written in specialized papers in different languages. Maria Gaetana integrated and clarified all this diverse information about calculus. These volumes were so well translated, compiled, and integrated that they became the standard calculus textbook in Europe for more than one hundred years. Maria Gaetana is thought to have begun this work as a textbook for her brothers and sisters.

This major effort was not purely the integration of others' work; Maria Gaetana added generalizations and methods of her own. Although she introduced many new ideas in her masterpiece, her name is often associated with a discovery that she shared with others: the formulation of what she called the *versiera*, a cubic curve. She had confused *versiera* with *versoria*, the term that Guido Grandi had given to the same curve. A literal translation of the colloquial Italian term *versiera* resulted in the word *witch*. Therefore, the curve has become known over the centuries as the *witch of Agnesi*.

Maria Gaetana not only wrote but also supervised the printing of *Analytical Institutions*. It was finished in 1748 on the presses of the Richini Publishing House. The presses were set up in her house, and the typesetters gained such valuable experience that they donated their services to Maria Gaetana's later publications. The two-volume work of more than one thousand pages was printed on handmade paper in large type with wide margins. It included large folios of etchings of analytic curves. Maria Gaetana dedicated this beautiful book to Empress Maria Theresa of Austria. The empress returned the kindness by giving the young mathematician lavish gifts: a crystal container, diamonds, and a diamond ring. Maria Teresa Agnesi had previously dedicated a volume of songs to the empress. The talented sisters felt honored to have so loving a patron.

Even before the publication of *Analytical Institutions*, Maria Gaetana had been elected a member of Accademia delle Scienze de Bologna, a society of scholars. It was a great honor. Because of her religious beliefs, Maria Gaetana was particularly pleased by Pope Benedict XIV's response to her book. He sent her jewels, but more important, he honored her by nominating her to a professorate at the University of Bologna, which was conferred on 5 October 1752. This recognition was personally significant to Maria Gaetana, although she never took the position.

After her father died in 1752, Maria Gaetana's life took a new direction. She gradually withdrew from scientific study and the very private work of the mathematician. She became devoted to theology and social work. She also continued to oversee the education of her younger brothers and sisters. Although she lived at home, she kept a rented apartment where she served the poor and sick of her parish. In 1759 she moved in with four people who needed care and sold her jewels—including her gifts from the empress of Austria—when she needed money to provide for them. During this time, she also taught religion to working-class individuals.

In 1771, Prince Antonio Toleneo Trivulzio donated his palace to be used as a home for the indigent aged. Cardinal Pozzobonelli asked Maria Gaetana to become the director of women at the facility, and she accepted. In 1783 she moved into the home, where she remained as director the rest of her life. In her later years, Maria Gaetana gradually became blind and deaf, and she suffered from spells of dropsy, the accumulation of fluid in the body. This condition brought on her death on 9 January 1799. In keeping with her wishes, Maria Gaetana was buried among the poor in a common grave.

Maria Gaetana Agnesi was a woman of exceptional quality and unusual achievement. She was recognized as the intellectual peer of men at a time when such recognition was rare. Unfortunately, many children's gifts of genius are neither recognized nor cultivated as Maria's were. Surely our world would be enriched if such gifts were developed.

Mary R. Monaco Lauck
Saint Matthew Cathedral School
South Bend, Indiana

Suggested Reading

Dictionary of Scientific Biography, s.v. "Maria Gaetana Agnesi."

Grinstein, Louise S., and Paul J. Campbell, eds. *Women of Mathematics: A Biobibliographic Sourcebook.* Westport, Conn.: Greenwood Press, 1987.

Kennedy, Hubert C. "The Witch of Agnesi—Exorcised." *Mathematics Teacher* 62 (October 1969): 480–82.

Perl, Teri H. *Math Equals: Biographies of Women Mathematicians + Related Activities.* Menlo Park, Calif.: Addison-Wesley Publishing Co., 1978.

Caroline Lucretia Herschel

—Merging New Mathematics with Astronomy

The mathematical developments of the late seventeenth and early eighteenth centuries made possible the important astronomical discoveries of the second half of the eighteenth century. The discovery of gravity by Isaac Newton and the formulation of calculus by Newton and Gottfried Wilhelm von Leibniz made possible the accurate calculation of the locations and paths of heavenly bodies. With these tools, astronomers were able to track heavenly bodies accurately and predict their movements and their positions at any time.

Caroline Herschel and her brother Frederick William benefited from, and built on, these discoveries. They are considered by many to be the parents of modern astronomy. Although Caroline also made observations and discoveries, William was the chief observer and Caroline was the recorder of the team's discoveries.

Caroline and William were descended from Hans Herschel, one of three brothers who left Moravia in the early part of the seventeenth century to escape the turmoil of the Reformation. Hans settled in Pirna, Saxony. His son, Abraham, was a gardener who worked at the court in Dresden. Abraham passed on to his youngest son, Isaac, a knowledge of arithmetic, writing, drawing, and music.

Isaac studied music and eventually moved to Hanover, where he became a bandsman in the Hanover Guards. He and Anna Isle Moritzen, whom he married in April 1733, had ten children. Caroline, the second youngest, was born in 1750. Only six of the children survived childhood.

It might have been said of Caroline that she started out as an ugly duckling without a future. As a child, she was disfigured as a result of smallpox. Her father feared that her physical appearance, combined with his inability to provide her with a dowry, made Caroline undesirable for marriage.

Isaac was, however, able to offer Caroline an intellectually stimulating family life. He wanted his children to be well educated. He was able to tend to their musical education himself. Caroline learned to read, write, and play the violin. Her interest in astronomy may have been inspired by her father. On clear nights, Isaac would take young Caroline out to observe the stars. Caroline learned the known constellations and was able to observe a comet.

A love of learning was evident in the Herschel home. In her memoirs Caroline recalls lying awake at night, listening to her father and oldest brothers, William and Jacob, in heated metaphysical discussions. Jacob thought that music was the only "science" worth learning, whereas William was interested in a variety of subjects.

Both Jacob and William had joined their father in the Hanover Guards. After the defeat in 1756 of the guards by French troops, Isaac sent his sons to England to escape France's forced exile of the Prussian troops. They settled in Bath, a health resort in the west of the country. From

October to Easter, wealthy people enjoyed the mild winter weather, the warm springs, and the social life in Bath.

William supported himself by giving music lessons and conducting concerts. He eventually became the organist for the Octagon Chapel, an elite private chapel in Bath.

Rheumatism and asthma brought on by wet battlefield conditions weakened Isaac and led to his death in 1767. The death of Caroline's father was a serious blow to her. With William gone, he had been the only significant man in her life. He had encouraged her to develop her gifts, but her mother and Jacob, who had returned to Hanover, considered her abilities limited. They thought of her only as a housekeeper and treated her like a servant. Anna did not value education as her husband had. She reluctantly accepted Caroline's proposal to attend school to learn to sew and embroider only because those skills related to Caroline's household chores.

William came to Caroline's aid. In 1771 he invited her to join him in Bath to replace the lead singer of concerts and oratorios. The move was resisted by Anna and by Jacob, who had been unsuccessful in establishing himself in England. In anticipation of her departure, Caroline made a two-years' supply of ruffles and socks for her mother and brother. Anna and Jacob finally agreed to the arrangement after William offered to pay for a servant to take Caroline's place.

William accompanied his sister to England. Hardship marked the trip. The first six days and nights were spent on the open seats of a mail coach. Caroline's hat blew away as they crossed the dikes in Holland. During the crossing of the English Channel, the boat lost its main mast and arrived off the English shore little more than a wreck. A sailor carried Caroline through the water and threw her onto the shore. The overland coach trip was not much better. One of the horses bolted, the carriage overturned, and Caroline was tossed from the coach.

Once in Bath, William arranged for Caroline to receive English, music, and arithmetic lessons. She also learned accounting and shopping to help her manage the household.

Caroline was not entirely happy in England. She was homesick and unfamiliar with the language. The artificial manners of the upper circles of society dismayed her, and she never really felt at home in Bath.

William's interest in astronomy was sparked indirectly by his love of music. His curiosity was aroused by *Harmonics*, a book written by Robert Smith, an astronomy professor at Cambridge University. This book explained the relationship between music and mathematics. Another book of Smith's, *A Complete System of Optics*, discussed astronomy and explained how to make a telescope.

Fascinated, William borrowed or rented telescopes to study the skies. He was not satisfied with their accuracy, however, so in 1773 he bought equipment for polishing and grinding lenses and started building his own telescope. Instead of *refracting* telescopes, which were in common use at the time, William began constructing *reflecting*, or *Newtonian*, telescopes. The reflecting telescope offered greater magnification and a clearer focus than the refracting telescope.

By manufacturing his own lenses and mirrors, William was able to produce instruments that were unmatched by those of his peers. Many of the distortions caused by the refracting telescopes were eliminated in William's instruments. The improved quality allowed William and Caroline to make more accurate astronomical observations.

William continued to teach music but also gave astronomy lessons. The entire Herschel house was turned into a laboratory. Different phases of telescope production took place in different rooms. In 1776 William completed his first twenty-foot telescope, with lenses and mirrors varying in size from four to twelve inches.

An acquaintance who was familiar with William's work introduced him to the Royal Society and to members of the royal court. King George III, a patron of the arts and the sciences, was so impressed with William's work that he made William the court astronomer in 1782. The stipend he received enabled William to stop conducting concerts and giving music lessons and to concentrate on astronomy.

Caroline was in demand as a vocalist. Although she felt that music was her true vocation, she gave up her music career to become William's assistant. She, too, received a stipend from the crown. For the first time, Caroline had an independent income.

Caroline and William moved to Datchet, near Windsor Castle, in 1782. The cost of maintaining a household was greater in Datchet than in Bath. Fortunately, word of William's superior telescopes had spread, and he was able to supplement the family income by selling his instruments. Caroline helped with the construction of telescopes and rekindled her childhood interest in astronomy.

In 1785 the Herschels relocated briefly to Clay Hall, a house near Windsor. After they discovered that the grounds of the home would not accommodate their twenty-foot telescope, they moved to nearby Slough in April 1786. The move was begun directly after the night's observations and completed swiftly so that the telescope could be set up for the following evening's observations. The telescope erected in Slough was used until 1813; it was not dismantled until 1839, seventeen years after William's death. In Slough Caroline was able to set up her own telescope and make her own observations.

After the move to Slough, William received a grant from the king to build a forty-foot telescope. This instrument was cumbersome, however, so the Heschels used it only for specific observations.

By the time that Caroline and William began to devote their energies entirely to astronomy, Newton and Leibniz had simultaneously discovered mathematical methods for calculating orbits. Pierre Simon de Laplace had demonstrated that the mechanism of the solar system could be deduced from the law of gravity. John Flamsteed's catalog of the positions of some three thousand heavenly bodies had been published by the Royal Society in 1725. Charles Messier had published his own catalog of forty-five nebulae (clouds of gas and dust) and galaxies in 1774; by 1780, he had discovered twenty-three additional nebulae.

The Herschels' work added considerably to the existing astronomical knowledge. Caroline recorded the observations William made during his four sweeps of the heavens. Fatigue, sleep, hunger, and cold were ignored by viewer and recorder. The Herschels took breaks only when the skies were not clear enough to view. Caroline spent the evenings recording; during the day she organized and rewrote the previous night's observations. Although Caroline downplayed her part in the team's efforts, she did all the numerical calculations and reductions. Her work was extremely accurate; no errors were found that could be attributed to her.

Caroline also sent notes about William's observations to the Royal Society and other interested parties. These detailed memoirs furnish the primary record of William's accomplishments. Caroline's cataloging of their discoveries established the Herschels' reputation as astronomers.

William's first sweep, begun in 1779, took two years to complete. In 1781 William discovered Uranus, the seventh known planet. This discovery had the effect of doubling the size of the known solar system. Uranus's distance from the Sun is about twice that of Saturn, which had previously been thought the farthest planet from the Sun. William submitted *Catalogue of Double Stars*, documenting 269 items, to the Royal Society in January 1782.

William Herschel was breaking new ground. He was the first to carry out the work necessary to prove the idea suggested earlier by Thomas Wright that the solar system is finite. William wondered if our star system might be just one of many that exist in the universe. He later discovered 848 double stars, and he was the first to demonstrate that gravitational forces functioned outside the solar system. William's observations and Caroline's mathematical calculations shattered the misconception that the stars are fixed in position or that they rotate around the earth.

Caroline began her own sweep of the heavens in 1782. In fall 1783 she found two nebulae. By the year's end, she had discovered fourteen nebulae.

From 1783 through 1785, William's second sweep resulted in the cataloging of 1000 new nebulae and clusters of stars. During this series of observations, he proved that the Sun and planets move together in space. He presented the proper motion of the Sun and the solar system to the Royal Society in 1783.

From December 1785 to 1788, William conducted an extensive third sweep of the skies, interrupting the sweep Caroline had begun in 1782. William's observations required instantaneous recording. William might sight six to twelve items a minute. Caroline described each item and recorded the longitude and latitude of its position. The resulting catalog added another thousand entries.

King George III asked William to accompany one of his telescopes to the University of Göttingen in July 1786. William's absence allowed Caroline to use the twenty-foot telescope herself. On 1 August 1786, she made her first discovery of a comet—comet 1786II.

The final sweep took place from 1788 through 1802. The Herschels persevered in this work for twelve hours a day. Caroline wrote in one of her recordings, "I have become entirely attached to the writing desk." Her persistence eventually resulted in a complete catalog of their observations.

In 1788 William married Mary Pitt. Although Caroline got along with Mary, she did not feel so close to her brother as she had before his marriage. Caroline moved into a cottage on the grounds of William and Mary's house that had been refurbished for her. After William's marriage, a ten-year gap appears in the detailed memoirs that Caroline had kept for years.

William's marriage, however, did not interrupt the Herschels' observations and recordings. William continued his third sweep, and in 1788, Caroline discovered her second comet—1788II. This comet, observed in 1939 by Roger Rigolet, bears the name Herschel-Rigolet.

By 1792, Caroline had observed four more comets. In 1795, she sighted a comet that she had been searching for since 1788. It had originally been observed by Pierre Méchain in 1786. Johann Franz Encke observed the same comet, which was then named for him, in 1819 and determined that the three astronomers had sighted the same comet.

Caroline made her final discovery of a comet on 6 August 1797. In little more than eleven years, she had discovered eight comets. This feat was not matched by another woman until Carolyn Shoemaker of the Palomar Observatory found her eighth comet in 1986, nearly two hundred years later.

William Herschel had noted major discrepancies between the data in Flamsteed's published catalog of 1725 and Flamsteed's unpublished notes of his original observations. At her brother's suggestion, Caroline cross-referenced the two catalogs. Caroline finished the *Index to Flamsteed's Observation of Fixed Stars* in twenty-two months and presented it to the Royal Society in March 1798. In addition, Caroline compiled a list of 560 stars not included in Flamsteed's catalog.

William completed his work in 1802. His final catalog contained some five hundred new listings. Over a nineteen-year period, he had observed and Caroline had recorded, organized, and cataloged approximately three thousand nebulae and star clusters. The Herschel catalogs became the foundation for the *New General Catalogue*, which is still used today.

Caroline continued to observe the heavens into the nineteenth century. She studied volcanoes on the moon and documented her last observation in 1811.

Around the time that William finished his work, Caroline became reacquainted with Mme Beckedorf, who had been a fellow student at Mme Kustner's sewing and dressmaking school in Hanover. Mme Beckedorf, a member of Queen Charlotte's household, introduced Caroline to the inner circle of the court at Windsor. Caroline began to spend with her friends the time she had previously devoted to astronomy.

After William died in 1822, Caroline, devastated by the loss of her partner and brother, returned to Hanover. Queen Charlotte had also died, the royal household had broken up, and Caroline's friends had begun to scatter.

Although Mme Beckedorf and her daughter also returned to Hanover, Caroline realized that the move to Hanover was a mistake.

William had left Caroline an annuity of 100 pounds. She also received a pension from King George IV. After the king died, the city of Hanover contributed to her support. Caroline turned over much of her money to her only surviving brother, Dieterich. Dieterich proved to be shiftless and irresponsible with Caroline's funds.

Caroline—at age seventy-three—began to catalog all William's nebulae and star clusters, arranging them by zones of one degree. When she completed the catalog in 1825, she sent it to William's son John, who was continuing his father's work. John presented the catalog to the Royal Astronomical Society (an offshoot of the Royal Society), which awarded Caroline a gold medal for her work.

John traveled to South Africa, arriving in Cape Town in 1834, to complete his father's cataloging of the heavens. Caroline was disappointed that her age prevented her from joining him to study the skies from the southern hemisphere. But she offered him suggestions about observing the constellation Scorpio.

At ninety-two, Caroline began a history of the Herschels' work. She was frequently visited by mathematicians and scientists who passed through Hanover. In honor of Caroline's ninety-sixth birthday, King Frederick William IV of Prussia presented Caroline with the Gold Medal of Science. With typical modesty, she demurred because she had not done any astronomical work for years.

This honor followed two other distinctions: In 1835, Caroline had been made an honorary member of the Royal Astronomical Society. The Royal Irish Academy then admitted her in 1836.

Caroline's last written communication was a letter she wrote to John on 3 December 1846. Caroline died on 9 January 1848, two months shy of her ninety-eighth birthday. She was buried next to her parents. Her love of astronomy is reflected in the epitaph she had prepared:

The eyes of her who is glorified
were here below turned to the
starry heavens.

James G. Murray
Brandywine Junior-Senior High School
Niles, Michigan

Caroline Lucretia Herschel   33

Suggested Reading

Hoskin, Michael A. "William Herschel and the Making of Modern Astronomy." *Scientific American*, February 1986, pp. 106–12.

Jefferys, William H., and Robert R. Robbins. *Discovering Astronomy*. New York: John Wiley & Sons, 1981.

Jones, Brian. "William Herschel: Pioneer of the Stars." *Astronomy* 16 (November 1988): 40–53.

Osen, Lynn M. *Women in Mathematics*. Cambridge: MIT Press, 1974.

Yeomans, Donald K. *Comets: A Chronological History of Observations, Science, Myth, and Folklore*. New York: John Wiley & Sons, 1991.

Sophie Germain

—Ahead of Her Time in Applied Mathematics

Determination is defined as the quality of being resolute—firm in purpose. It is a powerful attribute. If ever there was a woman with determination, it was Sophie Germain. She was born Marie Sophie Germain on 1 April 1776 in Paris, France, the daughter of Ambrose François and Marie Germain. The Germains were financially well off; Sophie's father was a silk merchant and a member of the bourgeoisie. Perhaps to avoid any confusion with her mother, Marie Sophie went by the name "Sophie." Born before the French Revolution, she grew up amid the social, economic, and political conflicts of late-eighteenth-century France. Sophie sought a serious purpose for her life. She neither married nor had children.

In Sophie's day women were not encouraged to pursue careers in mathematics. In fact, people deliberately discouraged the study of mathematics and science by women. The only women who received any academic education were those who had well-to-do parents.

These girls received some instruction from tutors. The opportunity to attend a school was reserved strictly for boys. The education of girls was limited, at best, to reading and writing. The study of literature was encouraged for young ladies, but the study of mathematics was off-limits for them. Most people thought that the probability of women's using their mathematical talents was remote, so a woman's study of mathematics seemed impractical.

During the economic, social, and political conflicts of late-eighteenth-century France, Sophie would spend time in her father's library, reading whatever she could find, since it was not safe for her to go outdoors. One day she came across a story about Archimedes, the Greek mathematician and inventor who discovered the laws of the lever and the pulley. Sophie read that when the Romans invaded Syracuse in the Greek colony of Sicily, Archimedes was down by the shore writing some mathematical figures in the sand. He was so engrossed in the mathematics problem he was working on that he never heard the Romans creep up on him, and he was killed. This story fascinated Sophie. She wondered what was so captivating about mathematics that it could command such profound concentration, especially from someone as intelligent as Archimedes. As a result, Sophie started reading books on mathematics.

Consequently, Sophie's parents began to worry about her. They believed that the study of mathematics was harmful for their daughter and discouraged her from pursuing it. Still, no matter what they did, she continued to read and study. They even went so far as to take all Sophie's candles and clothes and to put out the fire when they went to bed so she could not read books after bedtime. But these measures did not stop Sophie! She was about thirteen at this time, and already a very determined young lady. She did not argue with her parents or create a scene, but she did hide some candles in her room. After her parents went to sleep, she would get up, wrap herself in a quilt, take out the candles she had hidden, and work on math problems late into the night.

One morning Sophie's parents found her asleep at her desk, her paper filled with mathematics figures. It was extremely cold in her room, and the ink in her inkwell had frozen. Her interest in mathematics was so strong that it seemed nothing could stand in her way. What determination!

Finally, Sophie's parents realized that she had a "cause" that she was not going to give up easily. They loved her very much, so although they disapproved of her interest in mathematics, they finally compromised. They told her they would no longer stand in her way. They were willing to allow her to study mathematics, but they would not hire tutors to make it easier for her or help her out in any way. They were probably hoping that Sophie would soon outgrow her interest in mathematics. Eventually, realizing that this was not likely to happen, Sophie's mother secretly provided her with financial support.

Sophie was an intelligent young lady whose studies were not restricted to mathematics: she was interested in the relatively new field of psychology; she did some work in astronomy; she also taught herself Latin. Sophie continued her studies in mathematics beyond the study of algebra, which fascinated her. Sophie was interested in analyzing problems, and she also enjoyed developing mathematical arguments to support her analysis.

She read all she could by contemporary authors. In 1798 Adrien Legendre's essay on number theory drew Sophie's attention, and she began concentrating on this area of mathematics. She soon learned about a series of seminars that was being given by Professor Lagrange at the Ecole Polytechnique, an academy in France for the study of mathematics and science. Joseph Louis Lagrange was one of its first professors.

Because she was a woman, Sophie was not allowed to attend the seminars, but overcoming this obstacle was not difficult for her. She contacted some of her male friends who were attending the sessions at the academy and asked them to give her their notes. Sophie analyzed the notes on mathematics so well that she wanted to share her findings with the professor and the other men who were studying these concepts.

But how could she do so? At the end of each term, the students were required to submit a written report on their findings or contributions to the subject. When Sophie was eighteen years old, she wrote her analysis of the mathematical data and submitted it under the name "Monsieur LeBlanc." She decided to sign her report with a man's name because it was the only way her work would be read and taken seriously by the professor.

Professor Lagrange was quite impressed with Sophie's analysis. He wrote to Monsieur LeBlanc. When Lagrange finally discovered that "he" was really a "she," he encouraged Sophie to continue her studies and tried his best to have her contributions to mathematics recognized by other mathematicians. He also supported and encouraged her by supplying current information and data and by telling his friends about her. Fortunately, when some educated men of this era learned of a woman who excelled in the field of mathematics or science, they encouraged and assisted her. One practical way in which they helped Sophie was by sharing with her their comments on current mathematical topics.

Through Lagrange, Sophie became aware of the German professor Karl Friedrich Gauss, a well-known authority on number theory. At age twenty-five, Sophie decided to contact Professor Gauss and share some of her findings with him. She was even more hesitant to contact Gauss than she had been to approach Lagrange because Gauss was German.

During the early 1800s Germans were extremely reluctant to accept women in the field of mathematics—even more reluctant than mathematicians in other countries. Italians were probably the most accepting of women in this field. Next came the French, who were less comfortable with the idea of women in mathematics. However, they were not as prejudiced as the Germans. It was almost unheard of for a German to give any recognition to a woman in mathematics.

Sophie again used her pen name, Monsieur LeBlanc, when she corresponded with Gauss. She told Gauss that she was a student at the Ecole Polytechnique and that she shared his interest in number theory. Impressed with Sophie's observations, Gauss communicated with her for several years, never suspecting that Monsieur LeBlanc was really a woman.

During this time the revolutionary spirit was spreading, and France was preparing to invade the German states. Sophie became concerned about the safety of Karl Gauss. Remembering the legend of Archimedes, she was afraid that Gauss would be unaware of the dangers surrounding him. She contacted one of her family friends who was a general in the French army and directed him to give Gauss all the protection he needed. When the general contacted Gauss, he told him that Sophie Germain had asked him to protect Gauss from the French army.

Gauss had no idea who his protector was. After some discussion, he realized that the Monsieur LeBlanc with whom he had been communicating all this time was a woman named Sophie Germain. He was stunned. But to everyone's amazement, he became her patron. Through their correspondence, he encouraged her, and he did everything he could to help her continue her studies. Gauss's support of Sophie was remarkable, given the reluctance of the Germans to encourage women in mathematics.

Most of Sophie's early work dealt with number theory, a branch of pure mathematics. One particular number-theory problem Sophie worked with was Fermat's Last Theorem, which states that the equation $x^p + y^p = z^p$, where x, y, and z are nonzero integers, cannot be solved for p greater than 2. For example, when $p = 2$, we have $3^2 + 4^2 = 5^2$ and other well-known solutions. It is not difficult to understand this problem, but to prove the theorem is another matter. At the age of twenty-five, Sophie used analytic theory to construct a proof for p greater than 2 and less than 100. This result was an important accomplishment in mathematics. The theorem for all p greater than 2 appears to have been proved by Andrew Wiles in 1993.

At the turn of the century, mathematicians in France became intrigued with the work of the physicist Ernst Chladni. Chladni worked primarily with vibrations of elastic surfaces. Sophie, always one to keep up with new mathematical discoveries, became interested in applied mathematics as well as number theory. In her early thirties, she began to work with mathematics that had practical applications.

Sophie learned that a professor at the French Academy of Science had declared that a problem involving the vibration of elastic surfaces was unsolvable: When drumlike surfaces are sprinkled with fine powder and set vibrating, certain patterns appear in the powder. At that time mathematicians did not have any formula or mathematical basis for predicting the resulting patterns. This problem was so important to the French Academy of Science that a prize was promised to anyone who could solve it. To Sophie this problem was a challenge! Nothing was going to stop her from understanding and solving it. She worked day and night on it. Finally, after five years of work, Sophie thought she had come to a conclusion. When she was thirty-five years old, Sophie submitted an anonymous report of her results to the academy. Her work was rejected. Lagrange said that some of the findings were inadequate. The strong criticism of her work was difficult for Sophie to take, but she did not let it discourage her.

Sophie continued to work on the problem. Two years later, the academy held a second competition; again Sophie submitted a report. She was given an honorable mention for her work. This was a step in the right direction, but Sophie was still dissatisfied. She continued to work on the problem. She was on a mission. When she was forty years old, Sophie submitted a third report, this time under her own name. Her solution included a fourth-order partial differential equation. Finally, she experienced success! The French Academy of Science awarded Sophie a prize for her work on the vibrations of elastic surfaces.

In 1821, when Sophie's paper on the vibrations of elastic plates was published, Claude Navier, a well-known French mathematician, was so impressed with Sophie's power of analysis that he stated, "It is a work which few men are able to read and which only one woman was able to write." This tribute was an honor for women everywhere. Since that time, Sophie Germain has been considered one of France's greatest female mathematicians. At last she was invited to attend sessions at the

French Academy of Science. Her admission can certainly be considered the high point of her career and one of the greatest honors given to a woman of the era.

Karl Gauss told Sophie that he was impressed with her work. He did his best to have her recognized by the University of Göttingen and accepted as a professor on the faculty. He also hoped to have her awarded an honorary doctoral degree. Unfortunately, during this time Sophie developed breast cancer. She was about fifty-two years old. She suffered with cancer for more than two years. At the time not much was known about cancer, and people who were afflicted with the disease had little hope and had to deal with great pain. Sophie not only dealt with the pain but persevered in her studies. She continued her work in number theory, the elasticity of vibrating surfaces, and the curvature of surfaces.

Karl Gauss was delighted when he was finally able to convince the University of Göttingen to award Sophie an honorary doctorate, but regrettably, it was not conferred until a few months after Sophie's death. Although they had corresponded for years, Karl Gauss and Sophie Germain were never able to meet face-to-face.

Sophie died in 1831 at age fifty-five. One would think that after Sophie's death, the people of France would have officially honored her for her achievements. Not only had she received an honorary doctorate, but she had also made discoveries in both pure and applied mathematics. When a man of her distinction died, all his accomplishments were mentioned on his death certificate. Sophie's death certificate, however, did not mention any of her contributions to mathematics.

When the Eiffel Tower was completed in Paris in 1889, the names of all the individuals who were instrumental in erecting the tower were engraved on the cornerstone of the building. The principles that Sophie discovered about the elasticity of vibrating surfaces were necessary to the proper engineering of the tower. Without her work and the work of others who continued her studies, the building of the Eiffel Tower would not have been possible. It is unsettling to note that Sophie Germain's name was not included on the cornerstone.

But Sophie Germain's contributions were recognized by her colleagues—men as well as women. Mathematicians and scientists built on her work, and many of her struggles were rewarded. She succeeded in giving serious purpose to her life.

Elaine Bertolozzi Throm
Saint Matthew Cathedral School
South Bend, Indiana

Suggested Reading

Grinstein, Louise S., and Paul J. Campbell, eds. *Women of Mathematics: A Biobibliographic Sourcebook*. Westport, Conn.: Greenwood Press, 1987.

Mozans, H. J. *Woman in Science*. Notre Dame, Ind.: University of Notre Dame Press, 1991.

Osen, Lynn M. *Women in Mathematics*. Cambridge, Mass.: MIT Press, 1974.

Peri, Teri H. *Math Equals: Biographies of Women of Mathematics + Related Activities*. Menlo Park, Calif.: Addison-Wesley Publishing Co., 1978.

Mary Fairfax Somerville

6

—Life after Thirty as a Mathematician

Mary Fairfax Somerville was the author of four books that were both popular and important. Her first book, *Mechanism of the Heavens*, published in 1831, was a translation of a work by the French mathematician Pierre Simon de Laplace. England had become isolated from the ideas that were being developed on the European continent. This isolation was primarily caused by pride in Isaac Newton's discoveries. English mathematicians and scientists felt superior to their European counterparts. Mary Somerville's work brought Continental ideas to the people of England. She not only translated the work, she added her own observations. One of her goals was to make the work readable for a large population.

She described the concepts in language that was understandable, even to those with limited mathematical ability. Her work became a required textbook for honor students at Cambridge University in England.

Mary received high praise for her accomplishment. Dr. William Whewell, the master of Trinity College, wrote, "Mrs. Somerville shows herself in the field in which we mathematicians have been laboring all our lives, and puts us to shame" (Osen 1974, p. 110). As a result of her book's publication, Mary was elected a member of the Royal Astronomical Society in 1835, along with Caroline Herschel. Mary Somerville and Caroline Herschel were the first two women to receive this honor. The society placed a bust of Mary in its great hall. In addition, Mary received a pension of 200 pounds a year from the king of England.

Mechanism of the Heavens was published when Mary was fifty-one years old. The most remarkable thing about her mathematical ability is that she never received any formal training in mathematics. She did not start studying mathematics seriously until she was in her late teens.

Mary was born in Scotland on 26 December 1780, the daughter of Sir William Fairfax, a vice-admiral in the British navy, and Margaret Charters, the daughter of Samuel Charters, the solicitor of customs in Scotland. Mary lived a rather carefree life when she was a young girl. She grew up near the seacoast in the town of Burntisland and spent long hours combing the beaches. Her mother taught her to read the Bible and to say her prayers but gave her little other direction. Not much is known about the amount of instruction Mary received from her father in her early years. He is reported to have spent extended periods away from home on navy assignments.

When Mary was growing up, schooling in Great Britain was not mandatory. Each child's family was responsible for his or her education. Wealthy families usually taught their children reading and writing in their homes. If the family included male children, the parents would often hire a private tutor. Young girls would sometimes receive some attention from these tutors. But for the most part, girls were expected to be able to read novels, write letters, keep the household accounts, and do little else.

Mary's only formal schooling came when she was about nine years old and her father had returned after a long absence. He was not pleased that Mary was growing up to be a "savage." He sent her to a girls' school in Musselburgh, Scotland. Mary spent a year there; the experience was horrible. The headmistress of the school had very rigid notions about the proper education of young girls. Most of the schoolwork was tedious and included mindless memorization. This drill was coupled with a strict dress code that was supposed to help the girls become "ladies." Mary's description of their attire is vivid (Perl 1978, p. 85):

> I was enclosed in stiff stays with steel busk in front, while, above my frock, bands drew my shoulders back till the shoulderblades met. Then a steel rod, with a semi-circle which went under the chin, was clasped to the steel busk in my stays. In this constrained state I, and most of the younger girls, had to prepare our lessons.

Mary returned home and spent many hours reading books from the family library. Her mother allowed her to read, but Mary's aunt Janet, who lived with them, continually frowned on this activity. Aunt Janet once said, "I wonder you let Mary waste her time in reading; she never sews more than if she were a man." Mary's aunt reflected the views of the times about women's education.

When she was thirteen, Mary spent a summer in the town of Jedburgh, at the home of her uncle, Dr. Somerville. She had been trying to study Latin on her own and had become frustrated. Mary credited most of her difficulty to being a girl and therefore unable to learn. In response, her uncle told her of many ancient women who had been great scholars, and he agreed to tutor her in Latin. Mary spoke of these times as some of the happiest of her life.

When Mary was in her midteens, her life took an unexpected turn. She discovered a strange new area of mathematics—algebra. She was at a tea party in her hometown and was looking at some fashion magazines with a friend when she noticed some unusual symbols on the page. Here is her account of the story (Osen 1974, p. 100):

> At the end of the magazine, I read what appeared to me to be simply an arithmetical question, but on turning the page I was surprised to see strange-looking

lines mixed with letters, chiefly X's and Y's, and asked, "What is that?"

"Oh," said the friend, "it's a kind of arithmetic; they call it Algebra; but I can tell you nothing about it."

And we talked about other things; but on going home I thought I would look if any of our books could tell me what was meant by Algebra.

After returning home, Mary searched the books in the family library for any mention of algebra. She could find no information on this new subject. Mary later persuaded her youngest brother's tutor to purchase some simple texts on algebra and geometry. When the books arrived, Mary became absorbed in them. In the mornings and afternoons, Mary would play the piano and perform her womanly duties, but her evenings were devoted to studying mathematics. Unfortunately, Mary's parents were not supportive of her interest in mathematics. They believed, as did most people of the time, that it was unnatural for a girl to study mathematics. They had become aware of her zeal for studying when their servants complained about the dwindling supply of candles. Mary's parents promptly took away her stock of candles. Her father commented to her mother, "Peg, we must put a stop to this, or we shall have Mary in a straitjacket one of these days." This example further illustrates how the people of the time felt about women's learning mathematics.

In the years preceding her first marriage, Mary's life developed a pattern. She would rise early in the morning to read algebra and the classics before breakfast. Then she would practice the piano for five hours a day and afterward do her housework. Mary was no recluse; she led an active social life. She found time for gossiping with her friends and was fond of dancing. At times she would come home in broad daylight after dancing all night. Mary also loved the theater and attended many concerts.

In 1804 at the age of twenty-four, Mary married Samuel Grieg, a captain in the Russian navy. He, too, was unsupportive of her efforts to learn mathematics. The couple lived in London, where Samuel had been appointed Russian consul. During the next three years Mary had two sons; one died in infancy. After only three years of marriage, Mary's husband also died. Following Samuel's death in 1807, Mary returned to Burntisland. For the first time in her life, she was financially independent and was able to study mathematics and astronomy more intensely.

In 1812 she married her cousin William Somerville. Dr. Somerville was a surgeon in the British navy, and although quite intelligent, he had little personal ambition. He seemed more interested in Mary's achievements than in his own. At last Mary had found someone who was supportive of her work in mathematics and science. William helped her by searching libraries for books that she needed and by copying her manuscripts. During the next few years Mary and William had three daughters. Mary adjusted her daily routine to include their education.

Not long after her marriage to William, Mary obtained a set of books recommended by a friend who was a professor of mathematics at the University of Edinburgh. Mary was delighted (Osen 1974, p. 104):

> I was thirty-three years of age when I bought this excellent little library. I could hardly believe that I possessed such a treasure when I looked back on the day that I first saw the mysterious word "Algebra," and the long years in which I persevered almost without hope. It taught me never to despair. I had now the means, and pursued my studies with increased assiduity; concealment was no longer possible, nor was it attempted. I was considered eccentric and foolish, and my conduct was highly disapproved by many, especially by some members of my own family. They expected me to entertain and keep a gay house for them, and in that they were disappointed. As I was quite independent, I did not care for their criticism. A great part of the day I was occupied with my children; in the evening I worked.

To Mary these books were a rare treasure. For the rest of her life she would begin every day by studying mathematics. Still, she found time to rear her children, manage her home, and lead an active social life.

Because of William's position as head of the Army Medical Department, William and Mary had many friends. The couple spent time in London and lived near the Royal Institution of Great Britain. Here Mary continued her studies and came to know many intellectuals, including the naturalist Georges Cuvier; George Pentland, a naturalist and explorer; the mathematician Sir Charles Napier and his cousin of the same name, also a mathematician; the astronomers Caroline Herschel and Sir William Herschel; Dr. William Whewell; Henry Peter, Lord Brougham, a jurist; and the chemist and physicist Joseph Louis Gay-Lussac. She discussed astronomy and calculus with Pierre Laplace. Sir William Edward Parry, one of the leading astronomers of England and the Continent, was so impressed with Mary that he named a small island in the Arctic in her honor.

In 1827, after Mary had been studying mathematics for about thirty years, she received a request from Lord Brougham, a family friend, to translate the works of Laplace. Lord Brougham's initial request was made in a letter addressed to her husband. (It was not customary in Mary's time for the letter to be sent directly to her.) Mary was unsure of her ability to complete the task. She decided to attempt the work only after a personal visit from Lord Brougham. But Mary had one condition: Should she fail, no one would know of her attempt. Lord Brougham agreed. This work, *Mechanism of the Heavens*, was a major contribution to the advancement of mathematics in England.

In the years that followed, Mary completed three more major works: *Connection of the Physical Sciences*, *Physical Geography*, and *Molecular and Microscopic Science*. The latter was completed when she was eighty-nine years old.

As her life progressed, Mary continued to receive praise and admiration from many people in the fields of mathematics and science. Sir John Herschel, one of the most noted astronomers of the time, greatly admired Mary. Commenting on her award of the king's pension (addressing the letter to her husband, of course), Sir John wrote (Perl 1978, p. 90):

> Although the Royal notice is not quite so swift as the lightning in the selection of its objects, it agrees with it in this, that it is attracted by the loftiest; and though what she has performed may seem so natural and easy to herself, that she may blush to find it fame; all the rest of the world will agree with me in rejoicing that merit of that kind is felt and recognized at length in the high places of the earth. . . . I had almost forgotten that by a recent vote of the Astronomical Society I can now claim Mrs. Somerville as a colleague. Pray make my compliments to her in that capacity, and tell her that I hope to meet her there at some future session.

Ten years later Sir John Herschel wrote directly to Mary. He asked her to check out a powerful new telescope that an Italian colleague, DeVico, was using. Sir John trusted Mary's judgment even more than that of his enthusiastic colleague. He decided that Mary was the logical person to examine DeVico's claims about the telescope, since she was an authority in the field and was living in Italy at the time. Unfortunately, Mary was unable to do so because the telescope was located in the Collegio Romano, a monastery, which women were forbidden to enter. This ban presented a bitter irony—Mary was the most qualified person in Italy to judge the claims of DeVico, yet she was unable to do so because she was a woman.

Mary had to endure this type of discrimination her entire life, from her earliest attempts to learn about mathematics and astronomy to her exclusion from the Collegio Romano. As a result, she became a champion for the causes of minorities. She refused to use sugar in her tea during the American Civil War as an antislavery protest. She was further enraged when, after the Civil War, the emancipated slaves were given the right to vote but women were still denied this privilege. Mary was a strong supporter of women's rights. She once said, "Age has not abated my zeal for the emancipation of my sex from the unreasonable prejudice too prevalent in Great Britain against a literary and scientific education for women" (Perl 1978, p. 91).

Mary lived to be ninety-two years old. She died peacefully in her sleep in Naples in 1872. She was working on mathematics until the time of her death. She had never lost her ability to read or her interest in mathematics and science.

Mary Fairfax Somerville was a remarkable woman. She was born at a time when women were not afforded much in the way of education; what little education they received was limited to reading and writing. She was born into a society that frowned on the study of mathematics and science by women. She was ridiculed by members of her family and by her friends. She did not have any formal training and was unable to pursue mathematics at a early age. Because of her remarkable spirit, drive, and courage, she nevertheless persevered and overcame all these obstacles. Mary Somerville proved that women can achieve in mathematics and science, and she opened the doors to these fields for future generations of women.

George L. Lund, Jr.
The Stanley Clark School
South Bend, Indiana

Suggested Reading

Boyer, Carl B. *A History of Mathematics*. New York: John Wiley & Sons, 1991.

Mozans, H. J. *Woman in Science*. Notre Dame, Ind.: University of Notre Dame Press, 1991.

Osen, Lynn M. *Women in Mathematics*. Cambridge: MIT Press, 1974.

Perl, Teri H. *Math Equals: Biographies of Women Mathematicians + Related Activities*. Menlo Park, Calif.: Addison-Wesley Publishing Co., 1978.

Ada Byron Lovelace

7

—First Computer Programmer

Ada Byron Lovelace used her intellectual gifts and special talents to the fullest. Her mathematical genius allowed her to make a contribution that resulted in a great benefit to today's society—computer programming. Remarkably, this accomplishment was achieved during the nineteenth century, when British society imposed limitations on women.

Augusta Ada Byron, who was called "Ada," was born 10 December 1815. Her father was George Gordon Byron, Lord Byron, the celebrated British poet. Her mother was Anne Isabella ("Annabella") Milbanke, the only child of indulgent, middle-aged parents. The unlikely marriage of George Byron and Annabella lasted one year.

Three months after abandoning his wife and infant daughter, Lord Byron left his native country forever. He never saw Ada again, and Annabella raised her daughter alone.

Annabella did not resemble the usual debutante of her day. Determined to be a scholar, she preferred visiting museums and attending lectures to making festive social rounds. She was a born reformer. After reading Byron's *Childe Harold*, this sweet, earnest girl was not only concerned with the poet's moral welfare but was also determined to be his devoted friend. Thrilled by the thought of the challenge, Annabella believed it was her "duty to turn the brooding, libertine poet into a normal, cheerful" individual (Bigland 1956, p. 94). At the time, she did not suspect that Byron's nature had a darker, stormier side. Annabella had an idealistic image of him in her mind. For his part, Byron saw Annabella as an heiress and a prospective bride.

The marriage was doomed from the start. The dark side of Lord Byron's personality soon emerged. His behavior was erratic. At some moments he was fiercely temperamental. Then his mood would change, and he would brood. Byron took great pleasure in tormenting his new wife. His words to her were frequently harsh and cruel.

Annabella felt hurt, confused, and neglected. From the time of the honeymoon, she suspected that Byron was mad. Because of her suspicion, she engaged a doctor to examine her husband. When the doctor assured Annabella of Byron's mental soundness, she lashed back, "He may be mentally sound, but he is morally crazy."

Biographers agree that Byron's capricious moods resulted from his volatile childhood. Although both his parents were of high rank, their marriage proved unhappy, embittered, and embroiled by the debts and extravagance of Jack Byron, his father, and by the violent temper of Catherine "Kitty" Gordon, his mother. Byron had no memories of a happy, peaceful home. Lame because of a deformed foot, he had memories of an eccentric father who died when Byron was three years old and a cruel mother who hurled objects or venomous taunts at him. "Lame brat" was one name that hurt Byron deeply. That Lord Byron never became a steady, well-respected family man should therefore be no surprise: the marriage of Lord Byron and Annabella never veered off its destructive path.

After the birth of Augusta Ada, Byron did nothing to settle the upheaval in the Byron household. Annabella felt compelled to share her suspicions of her husband's mental illness with her parents. As a result, the relationship between Byron and his in-laws became understandably cool. Thirty-six days after Ada's birth, Byron sent his wife and daughter to visit his in-laws. He suggested that they stay with the Milbankes until his financial situation improved. Annabella was devastated by her husband's behavior.

The brief period after Ada's birth was the only time the poet ever saw his daughter. But Annabella lived in fear that her husband would demand custody of their child, which in England was the right of the natural father. Occasionally, Byron threatened to take Ada from Annabella and to have her raised by his sister Augusta, but he never acted on these threats.

Sadly, because of Byron's deplorable behavior, Ada was not even allowed to see her father's portrait for many years. When Ada was only eight years old, the father she never knew died in Greece. Ironically, on his deathbed he wrote a letter to Augusta, asking for news of the daughter he had abandoned years earlier.

Ada once wrote to her mother that she would like to compensate humanity for her father's "misused genius" (Huskey and Huskey 1980, p. 310):

> If he has transmitted to me any portion of that genius, I would use it to bring out great truths and principles. I think he has bequeathed this task to me. I have this feeling strongly; and there is a pleasure attending it.

These words may seem rather curious for a girl raised in Victorian England, where education for females of Ada's rank included the social graces, music, painting, and foreign languages. However, life for Lord Byron's daughter was multifaceted. Like other young women of her class, Ada spent the winter season in London. While there, she devoted her time to attending concerts, theater performances, and parties. On 10 May 1833 Ada was presented at court. The occasion was followed by a series of court balls.

Unlike her peers, however, Ada devoted time to the study of mathematics. She was encouraged by her mother, a learned woman in her own right, who herself had more than an average interest in the subject. In fact, Byron once referred to his wife as the "Princess of Parallelograms."

Ada's mathematical genius was recognized when she was very young. When she was five, her governess observed that Ada correctly added sums of five or six rows of figures. At the age of ten, Ada informed her mother that she was working hardest at Italian and arithmetic. And before she was thirteen, Ada was studying geometry.

Undoubtedly, Ada was better off not attending a school where she would have been obliged to follow the typical curriculum for young ladies of her class. Living a sheltered life among her mother's circle of friends, Ada was better educated through governesses, tutors, and, later, independent study.

Since mathematics was her passion, Ada was fortunate to be able to meet Charles Babbage and Mary Somerville when Ada was growing up. Mary Somerville was famous for several mathematics and science books she had written. Ada frequently accompanied Mary to Charles's Saturday evening parties during the London social season. It was during one of these parties that Ada first became acquainted with him.

Charles Babbage was an eminent scientist and mathematician and a prolific inventor. His inventions include the speedometer, the skeleton key, the locomotive "cow catcher," and the ophthalmoscope, which doctors use to examine the retina of the eye. He was a fellow of the Royal Society and held the same chair at Cambridge that Britain's most famous scientist, Isaac Newton, once occupied.

As a mathematician, Charles Babbage found numerous errors in the handwritten mathematical table he used to solve polynomial equations. As a scientist and inventor, he believed he could build a machine to solve polynomial equations more easily and accurately. He envisioned a machine that would not only calculate but also automatically print the entries in tables.

Charles created a demonstration model of his difference engine. It worked by solving what mathematicians call "difference equations." Ada Byron, then in her late teens, is said to have understood how the difference engine worked as soon as she saw it during an early visit to Charles's studio.

Contrary to what its name implies, the machine constructed tables using repeated additions, not subtractions. The word *engine* comes from the same Latin root as *gignere*, which means to beget. Originally, *engine* meant any clever invention. Later it came to mean "a machine that converts heat energy into mechanical work."

The model of the difference engine was so well received that the project was funded with a grant from the British government, and Charles Babbage began to build a full-scale working version. Unfortunately, he ran into difficulties and had to abandon the project after the British government withdrew its financial support.

Charles was not discouraged. The setback was only temporary because he conceived what he thought was a much better idea. Inspired by Joseph Marie Jacquard's punch-card-controlled loom that was programmed to weave patterned fabrics, Charles envisioned a punch-card-controlled machine that he hoped would perform many kinds of calculations. He named his new invention the "analytical engine."

Because the British government had sunk thousands of pounds into the difference engine and had received no return on its investment, the government had no intention of making the same mistake with the analytical engine. Therefore, Charles did not build a working, full-scale version. This early computer remained only an idea because technology was not sophisticated enough to make the analytical engine a reality, since no power source was available. The analytical engine's design, however, featured many characteristics of modern computers:

1. An input device
2. A storage facility that saved data
3. A processor that carried out arithmetic calculations

4. A control unit that directed the machine to carry out instructions
5. An output device

Even though no working version of the design was constructed, Ada used the mathematical talent inherited from her mother and the writing genius inherited from her father to develop instructions for doing computations on Babbage's analytical engine. Her work was the forerunner of computer programming.

Ada began working with Charles Babbage on a translation project when she was in her midtwenties and married to William King, Lord Lovelace. Ada was her husband's intellectual superior—a fact that he did not seem to mind. William was proud of his wife's accomplishments in mathematics and encouraged her collaboration with Charles Babbage.

The task undertaken by the two was to translate a paper describing the function and theory of Charles Babbage's analytical engine written by L. F. Menebrea, an Italian mathematician and ambassador to France. Ada proposed that she translate the paper from French so that English readers could learn from it.

The undertaking proved to be more involved than initially thought. The original work was expanded because of Ada's annotated translation and the series of accompanying notes. Since the new text was far superior to the original, Charles thought it should be published as an original paper. Ada disagreed, preferring to honor her commitment to the publisher, which was to translate Menebrea's text.

During the course of the project, Ada's confidence grew. Recognizing her own competence and contributions to the work, she became upset when Charles was careless—losing material, forgetting to make corrections, or making revisions in her work without her permission. Inevitably, their working relationship became strained.

When the project was finally completed, Ada was torn. She wanted to receive credit for her work, yet women of her rank did not write papers—especially in mathematics and science. She decided that the best course of action was to sign "A. A. L." to the completed work. Only a few close friends and family members knew that A. A. L. was Lady Lovelace. The identity of the translator of Menebrea's work was kept a secret for some thirty years.

Ada Lovelace and Charles Babbage never again worked together on a similar project. Because of Charles's careless work habits and lack of organizational skills, Ada set down certain conditions that he would have to honor if he desired to use her expertise in future endeavors. This arrangement was aimed at avoiding the strain and arguments they had experienced during the Menebrea project. Charles penciled this note across the top of the letter outlining the conditions under which Ada would work with him: "Morning 15, Saw AAL this morning and refused all the conditions."

Eventually the hard feelings that had developed during the collaboration on the Menebrea project were smoothed out. The Babbages and Lovelaces remained close family friends.

The second collaboration between Ada and Charles involved testing mathematical theories of probability. They devised what they expected to be an infallible system to beat the odds when betting on horses. Charles saw the system as a solution to his mounting financial difficulties. Most of his personal funds had been invested in his still unfinished difference engine. Unfortunately, the project ended disastrously—especially for the Lovelaces.

When William realized that the system did not work, he stopped gambling. He assumed that his wife had quit as well. But unlike William and Charles, Ada continued to gamble. The reason she continued betting is unclear. Eventually, she fell deep into debt. Ada's family were not at first aware that she had lost large sums of money. On two occasions she was forced to pawn the family jewels, which Annabella redeemed both times.

Ada's actions not only caused her husband and mother a great deal of anguish but also destroyed their close family relationship. Annabella accused William of failing to take proper care of his wife. She also held him accountable for Ada's gambling. William, for his part, was infuriated because he had not been told that Ada had pawned the family jewels. To make matters worse, Ada's health had declined.

Worried by Ada's suffering, William hoped that his mother-in-law's presence would do his wife good, so he allowed Annabella to help with the Lovelace household. Once established there, Annabella prohibited Charles Babbage from ever seeing her daughter again. She upheld her decision even though Ada's doctors advised William that it would be callous to prevent his wife from seeing her former colleague.

Ada's illness was later diagnosed as cancer. After months of suffering, Lady Lovelace died on 27 November 1852. She was thirty-six years old, the same age her father had been when he died. At her request, Ada was buried next to him in the Byron family vault at Hucknall Torkard Church in Nottinghamshire, where his body had been laid to rest since its return from Greece.

The identity of the translator of the Menebrea project has been revealed to the general public. As computers continue to have an impact on our society, the work of Ada Lovelace has been reexamined. Because of her text outlining the repeated use of a set of cards that have a purpose similar to that of the subroutines in today's computer programs, she is credited with being the first computer programmer. Ada Lovelace was prophetic when she advised against overrating computers. She understood the machine's shortcomings. She wrote the following (Perl 1978, p. 108):

> The Analytical Engine has no pretensions whatever to originate anything. It can do whatever we know how to order it to perform. It can follow analysis, but it has no power of anticipating any analytical revelations or truths. Its province is to assist us in making available what we are already acquainted with. Any thinking which the machines do indeed do must be put in. They must be programmed to think and cannot do so for themselves.

In retrospect, that Ada Lovelace compensated humanity for her father's "misused genius" has been decided by those who chose to honor her contributions by naming a new programming language *Ada*.

Karen Nilson
North School
Watervliet, Michigan

Suggested Reading

Bigland, Eileen. *Passion for Excitement: The Life and Personality of the Incredible Lord Byron.* New York: Coward McCann, 1956.

Capron, Harriet L. *Computers, Tools for an Information Age.* Menlo Park, Calif.: Benjamin/Cummings Publishing Co., 1987.

Graham, Neill. *Mind Tool.* Saint Paul, Minn.: West Publishing Co., 1986.

Huskey, Velma R., and Harry D. Huskey. "Lady Lovelace and Charles Babbage." *Annals of History of Computing* 2 (October 1980): 299–329.

Perl, Teri H. *Math Equals: Biographies of Women Mathematicians + Related Activities.* Menlo Park, Calif.: Addison-Wesley Publishing Co., 1978.

Thomas, Henry, and Dana Thomas. *Living Biographies of Great Poets.* Garden City, N.Y.: Blue Ribbon Books, 1946.

Maria Mitchell

—Early American Astronomer

Long ago, people were terrified when a comet trailed across the sky. They thought it signaled the end of the world. Now, people are no longer frightened by a comet's appearance, but they do find comets awe inspiring.

A comet first appears as a bright, hazy spot in the sky. It can appear to rise and set like the stars or move slowly along a course of its own. Gradually, a filmy tail stretches out from the haze; it is made of matter so thin that stars can be seen through it, and it may become millions of miles long. After a while, a starlike nucleus appears in the middle of the comet's "head," which comprises clusters of gaseous matter held together by gravitational pull.

After the telescope was invented, astronomers were able to observe comets carefully. Traveling in long orbits, comets were found to be as large as, or larger than, planets. A comet becomes visible when it loops close to the sun. Then it swings away and gradually disappears.

If its orbit is open, the comet goes off into space, never to be seen again. If its orbit is closed, the comet will probably return.

Maria Mitchell became well known when she discovered a "new" comet through her telescope. On 1 October 1847 Maria spotted Mitchell's comet, aptly named after her, from atop the homemade observatory built onto the roof of her house. It was not unusual for Maria to be watching from the white-railed platform, her telescope fixed on the horizon. Maria, like many New England residents, loved the stars.

Maria was born in 1818 on the beautiful island of Nantucket, thirty miles from Cape Cod, Massachusetts. Nantucket was settled in 1659 by Quakers whose main occupations included shipbuilding and fishing. By the early nineteenth century, this fifteen-mile-long island had become a major whaling center, accommodating more than one hundred twenty-five seafaring vessels in its port. Nearly everyone in this whaling town was in the habit of observing the heavens—it was part of the way of life. It may have been the spirit of Nantucket that stimulated Maria's love for the stars.

Maria was the third of ten children. Because the Mitchells were Quakers, one might imagine that their family life was staid and serious, but Maria's family was somewhat unconventional by traditional Quaker standards. For example, the Sabbath was to be strictly observed by Quakers; on this day even laughter was forbidden. But in the Mitchell house the children were allowed to play in the attic on the Sabbath (as long as the neighbors could not hear them). Over the years the family bent other rules, and the Quaker elders told the Mitchells to beware, for the devil was leading them into sin.

As the years passed, both Maria and her father continued to be pulled between their personal beliefs and the beliefs of the Quaker faith. To his children's delight, Mr. Mitchell even allowed a piano into their home. This act caused quite a stir in the Quaker community, but Mr. Mitchell knew that in time the criticism would pass.

Even though Maria became one of America's great scientists, she began her education as a poor student. She entered Nantucket's first public school at age nine and simply could not learn the lengthy "laundry lists" that students in her day were required to memorize. Eventually, Mr. Mitchell started his own school, which was more to Maria's liking. She was able to take time to watch—and wonder.

Of all the family members, Maria was closest to her father and her older brother, Henry. When Henry ran away and joined the crew of a whaler, Maria looked on sadly as he packed his knapsack. She was left with only her memories of him and the beauty of the stars that linked them together.

Maria struggled to do her needlework and chores when she would rather have been on the rooftop, stargazing with her father. She also enjoyed mathematics. One night when she attempted to solve the problems her father had assigned, she could find no quiet place to work. (With so many other Mitchell children about, it was no wonder.) So Mr. Mitchell surprised her by turning the upstairs closet into her personal study. Afterward, she could be found there whenever she had a free moment or when the clouds hid the stars. She loved solving geometry and trigonometry problems.

One evening while preparing to view an eclipse, Maria and her father attempted to take the telescope onto the roof. The February wind would not allow them to hold the telescope steady, so their plans had to be canceled. So that they would not miss the eclipse entirely, they removed the parlor windows and were able to see the annular eclipse of the sun from inside the house. Their passion to scan the heavens was so intense that the entire household came to a standstill while father and daughter indulged their interest in astronomy.

Her father's influence had much to do with the development of Maria's personality. A man of many interests and talents, Mr. Mitchell earned his living in various ways. Over the years he was employed as a cooper (one who makes wooden barrels), a schoolmaster, and a bank officer. As an amateur astronomer, he was hired by whalers to rate their chronometers.

Chronometers, or ships' clocks, needed to be checked for accuracy by means of stellar observations. One night while Maria's father was away, a ship's captain came to have his chronometer rated so that he could sail the next morning. Young Maria did not want to turn the captain away for fear that her father would lose future jobs. She convinced her older sister to assist her while Maria spent most of the night with a sextant and a telescope, making the intricate calculations necessary to rate the chronometer. In the morning her father arrived home and checked her calculations. They were exact. When her father asked whom the captain should pay, Maria obligingly replied, "He who taught me."

When Maria was sixteen, she ended her formal education and opened her own school. It was quite unconventional according to Nantucket standards. Quaker beliefs upheld education for all; in practice, however, Portuguese or black children were not permitted to enter the Quaker schools. But in Maria's school, all children were welcomed. This practice, of course, was frowned on by Nantucket residents.

At age seventeen Maria was offered a job as librarian of the new Nantucket Athenaeum. This position gave her plenty of time for study. It also enabled her to influence young people's reading. Even as a librarian, she could not escape her yearning to remain a teacher. When Maria found a child avidly reading a book, she in turn would read it to see if she found it appropriate. Maria censored material that went against her strict Quaker standards. Many books that did not meet her standards were found by library patrons to be missing from the shelves. At the annual inventory the trustees would, of course, discover the books on the shelves, but afterward they would again disappear.

Maria discovered Mitchell's comet while she was employed as a librarian. She was twenty-eight years old. King Frederic of Denmark had offered gold medals to the first observers of "telescopic" comets. Perhaps winning a medal was Maria's goal each night as she scanned the heavens. At her father's instigation and after considerable correspondence, King Frederic awarded Maria a gold medal. She received the medal exactly one year after she had discovered the comet. Maria Mitchell immediately became famous. She was the first female American astronomer; some called her the Astronomeress.

In 1848, the year she received the medal, Maria became the first woman elected to the prestigious American Academy of Arts and Sciences. Amid controversy, she emerged as a symbol for women in science and mathematics. Many of the nation's scientists thought that women had no place in a society of scholars. They contended that women did not have the nature or the intelligence needed for serious study. But Maria was elected anyway. Not until ninety-five years later was the next woman admitted to the academy.

In 1850 Maria was unanimously elected the first female member of the American Association for the Advancement of Science. She immediately became very involved and began to fight for women's right to pursue scholarship.

While working as a librarian, Maria was also employed to do mathematical calculations for the *Nautical Almanac*, an important American version of tables of basic data about the heavenly bodies. She continued working with these calculations for many years, although she received only $500 a year for this part-time job.

Eventually Maria's father suggested that she leave the library and accept a tutoring job that would allow her many opportunities to travel. Taking his advice, Maria became a world traveler and met many famous people, including the astronomer Sir John Herschel, the mathematician Mary Somerville, and the novelist Nathaniel Hawthorne. She visited the Royal Observatory, a far cry from her little perch on her roof, and requested and received permission to see the famed Collegio Romano, the prestigious monastery observatory in Rome. The Collegio Romano had previously banned women from the premises, including Caroline Herschel and Mary Somerville.

On returning from Europe and its fascinating sights and places, Maria discovered that her mother was dying. Death was already too familiar to Maria—two of her male astronomer friends had passed away, and she had recently lost her nephew to smallpox. Her father had always told her to "seek solace in the stars," and she took this advice to heart when her mother died. Soon after, Maria and her father moved to Lynn, Massachusetts, to be closer to other family members. Maria continued her work and published several articles on comets and double stars.

One day a representative of Matthew Vassar visited the Mitchells. Vassar was building a women's college in New York State, and he hoped that Maria would accept a position there as professor of astronomy. Maria initially felt she could not accept because she lacked a college degree. Her father again came to her aid, reminding her of the honorary degree granted to her in 1853 by Hanover College. Mindful of this honor and further encouraged by her father, Maria happily accepted this important new position.

Unfortunately, in the 1860s many others did not share Vassar's enthusiasm for women in higher education, a new idea at that time. Disregarding the controversy, Maria and her father set up their living quarters in Vassar's observatory, which had been prepared especially for her. In fall 1865, Maria Mitchell, astronomer, welcomed some three hundred young ladies to the first day of classes. She addressed her students enthusiastically during her first lecture in the observatory, speaking with such passion that morning that she forgot the notes intended to help her. Her young audience was spellbound by this pioneering educator. No one moved, even when the bell rang to end the class.

Just as she had done at age seventeen, Maria used unconventional approaches to education. She was not fond of the many rules governing the behavior of the students at Vassar. She particularly disliked the rules that forbade students to leave their rooms after 10:00 P.M. and that required the young ladies to change from cotton to silk gowns for dinner. Sometimes Maria's disdain for rules and regulations got her into trouble. Late one night Maria roused her young students from bed to observe a meteor shower, the likes of which would not be seen again for thirty-three years. When chastised by the principal for the disruption, Maria calmly replied that it was a shame that the heavens above had not planned the event at a more suitable time of day.

On another occasion, watching with her students late one night, Maria noticed a dying apple tree blocking the best view of a comet. She quickly found the school's handyman and had him cut down the tree. The next day Maria's class called her "George Washington." There was never a dull moment for people who were around Maria Mitchell.

About this time, grief struck again when Maria's beloved father passed away. But she had so much to do, between her work in the classroom and the observatory, that Maria knew her father would want her to carry on; and so she did.

Soon Maria was approached to join in the growing public movement for women's rights, another idea that was new for the times and often unpopular. But Maria was not ready to join the cause until she traveled again, this time to Russia. There she noticed that women voted and that they received equal pay for equal work—conditions that did not exist in America.

Maria's observations encouraged her to try to make changes when she returned to the United States. She discovered that women were getting paid less than men at Vassar. This situation angered her. She believed that it was not only a denial of women's equal rights but a blow against the college's goal to elevate women. Maria complained to the president of Vassar, but she was not satisfied with his response. When Professor Mitchell announced that she and the other female teachers would be forced to leave the next day, the president quickly adjusted the pay scale.

In 1873 Maria traveled to New York City with a Vassar colleague. Along with many other outstanding women, they formed the Congress of Women. Maria served as its first vice-president. Three years later she was elected the group's president. One of the first issues raised by the congress was voting rights for women. Maria Mitchell believed that someday the struggle for equality of the sexes would lead to an even greater struggle: the struggle for the equality of all people.

During her adult years, Maria sometimes questioned God's existence and omnipotence. She liked the doctrines of peace and love taught by the Quaker religion but did not adhere to its confining disciplines. In time Maria was disowned by her Quaker church. Thereafter, she attended the Unitarian Universalist church; however, she never became a member. Her refusal to join any church was thought of as ungodly at Vassar. Once a chapel service at Vassar College ran too long for Maria's liking, nearly interfering with an observation of Saturn she had planned. The predictable Mitchell response was a letter to the president of the college requesting shorter prayers!

During the last part of her life, Maria enjoyed considerable prestige. She was respected by her fellow scientists, magazine writers toasted her, and she received numerous distinctions. In addition to the gold medal from the king of Denmark, she received two honorary degrees, one from the aforementioned Hanover College in 1853 and another from Columbia University in 1887. Maria also received an honorary doctorate from Rutgers Female College. Besides these honors, a public school in Denver is named for her, as is a crater on the moon. Maria's name can also be found on the front of the Boston Public Library. Following her death, the Maria Mitchell Association of Nantucket, a civic-minded organization that honors her principles, was established.

Even given Maria's many achievements, it is probable that an individual living in Poughkeepsie or Cape Cod would not have heard of her. Unfortunately, to this day lesser male astronomers and scientists are written about in history books, to the exclusion of notable women. Maria wrote of her life (Baker and Baker 1962, p. 65), "The best that can be said of my life so far is that it has been industrious, and the best that can be said of me is I haven't pretended to be what I was not."

Maria's published works show her to be an observer and a teacher rather than a scholarly, theoretical astronomer. This choice was deliberate. Although her devotion to teaching hampered and limited her time for research, Maria firmly believed that teaching and research were two different fields and could not be simultaneously pursued.

Maria retired on Christmas Day in 1888. After twenty-three years of teaching, she had her last "dome party" (the annual dome parties had been held in the observatory; all the food was shaped like stars and crescents.) Maria's student assistant, Mary Whitney, followed in her mentor's footsteps and became Maria's successor. Maria Mitchell died in Lynn,

Massachusetts, in 1889. Her final words were, "If this is dying, there is nothing unpleasant about it." Maria will be remembered as a great woman in science and as an advocate of women's rights and women's higher education.

Mary R. Monaco Lauck
Saint Matthew Cathedral School
South Bend, Indiana

Suggested Reading

Baker, Rachel, and Merlen Baker. *America's First Woman Astronomer.* New York: Julian Messner, 1962.

Gersh, Harry. *Women Who Made America Great.* Philadelphia: J. B. Lippincott Co., 1962.

Mozans, H. J. *Woman in Science.* Notre Dame, Ind.: University of Notre Dame Press, 1991.

Rubin, Vera. "Women's Work." *Science,* July–August 1986, pp. 58–64.

Stoddard, Hope. *Famous American Women.* New York: Thomas Y. Crowell Co., 1970.

Wilkie, Katharine E. *Maria Mitchell, Stargazer.* Champaign, Ill.: Garrard Publishing Co., 1966.

Florence Nightingale

—Nurse, Statistician, Reformer

With the birth of their second daughter in May 1820, William and Fanny Nightingale decided to end the extended honeymoon they had enjoyed in Europe. They returned home to England with their infant daughters, Parthenope and Florence, both named for the cities in which they had been born. Lea Hurst, the Nightingales' summer home in Derbyshire, was at its loveliest at the time of their arrival. Perched high on a windy hill and surrounded by terraced gardens, it was bordered by the River Derwent. It was the perfect place to spend the hot summer months. The Nightingales looked forward to spending many summers at Lea Hurst, watching their daughters grow and enjoying the lifestyle their wealth afforded them.

The family spent the winter months at Embly Park in Hampshire, a beautiful estate surrounded by wide lawns and gardens. With many servants, a nurse, and a nursery maid to tend the girls, life was nearly perfect for the Nightingales. They entertained a constant stream of the British social elite. Both foreign and domestic dignitaries were entertained at Embly Park. Florence and Parthenope formed close relationships with some of Europe's most influential people.

Parthenope, a rather plain young woman, loved the parties, balls, and entertaining that filled England's winter social season. She liked nothing more than helping her mother arrange flowers or plan enticing menus for their guests. She also enjoyed dressing up in formal attire.

Parthenope's younger sister, Florence, was her opposite in many ways. With red-gold hair and a flawless complexion, Florence was beautiful and attracted a great deal of attention. But she was painfully shy and preferred the company of her academically minded father. She loved books, reading, and the challenge of learning. Much of her time was spent mending broken dolls, writing prescriptions for them, or tending to the minor wounds of various animals. Parthenope and her mother were never able to understand Florence's shyness or her disregard for the social amenities they found so vital.

The Nightingale family and their relatives often visited one another when the girls were growing up. Many times Florence was asked to help care for a sick cousin or a colicky newborn. Even as a child, she seemed to have a way with her patients.

Mr. Nightingale eventually took over the girls' lessons. As a teacher, he was patient and kind. Florence thoroughly enjoyed studying Greek and Latin. Her natural gifts for languages and statistics especially pleased Mr. Nightingale. She devoured Greek literature and loved translating it. Her mind sang with German, Italian, and French poetry. Parthenope, however, struggled through any lessons that required strict concentration and mental discipline.

As she matured, Florence grew increasingly frustrated with her mother and sister. Florence could not understand them, and they could not understand her. The only peaceful moments Florence spent with her mother were on Mrs. Nightingale's regular visits to local sick and needy families. Because of these visits, Florence was able to see the vast difference between her world and that of the British commoner. On these trips she became aware that the streets were filled with people wrapped in thin, ragged blankets as their only protection from the biting winter winds and she saw children standing bare-foot in icy puddles. She could not forget the tiny, windowless cottages; the fetid odor and filth; or the gaunt, hollow-eyed children with runny noses who were present at each stop. Florence knew that the small portions of food and medicine they brought to these unfortunate families would not be of substantial help. She also knew there had to be a better way to help relieve the suffering of the poor—some way to make a real difference!

Florence became consumed with finding a way to serve these throngs of people; they seemed to be everywhere. But her age, gender, and social standing were barriers that Florence felt unable to breach. She became more and more resentful with the passing of each social season—filled with dinners and parties—that so many people went to bed cold and hungry. In her growing frustration, Florence began a quiet rebellion. She refused any social obligation that took time away from what she considered to be more important. Mrs. Nightingale and Parthenope were equally frustrated with Florence. Eventually, Mrs. Nightingale had to accept the fact that her younger, more beautiful daughter was very different from Parthenope and other young ladies of their age.

One winter evening, when Florence was seventeen, she heard a heavenly voice as she prepared for bed. This voice was the inspiration she needed to clarify her vision. She entered this remark in her journal: "On February 7, 1837, God spoke to me and called me to his service" (Cosner 1988, p. 21).

The Nightingales spent the next two years in Europe, finishing the girls' education. Florence became closer to her family and was less agitated during this period. After the family's return to England in 1839, Florence was presented to British society and to the young Queen Victoria. Neither young woman could know, as they smiled at each other that evening, that they would meet again as great and noble women. Each would do her part to change history and benefit humankind.

After her presentation at court, Florence became the reigning British debutante. Beautiful and charming, she was the belle of every ball and was beleaguered by suitors. Her days and nights were spent in a whirlwind of dinners, plays, concerts, and parties. Florence enjoyed all the attention she received, until she remembered God's charge to her. She wrote in her journal, "All that poets sing of the glories of this world seem to me untrue. All the people I see are eaten up with care or poverty or disease" (McKown 1966, p. 54). She never again lost sight of her intention to somehow make a difference in the lives of the unfortunate.

The arguments in the Nightingale family resumed as Florence rejected suitor after suitor, preferring instead to remain home caring for sick relatives or poor villagers. Her stubborn refusal to trade the nursing care she provided to a growing circle for dinners, balls, and the theater was beyond the understanding of her mother and sister. They were humiliated and could not begin to explain Florence or her obvious disdain for British social tradition. For her part, Florence grew tired of trying to explain and defend what she felt compelled to do. There was much to do, but she knew she was limited by her ignorance.

British hospitals at that time were dark, suffocating, filthy prisons of neglect. Their floors and walls were covered with slime. The beds were lice infested, and the nurses, for the most part, were promiscuous drunkards. These hospitals were houses of death; people were sent to them only to die. The Nightingales forbade Florence even to set foot in a hospital, particularly because of the low class of women she would be working with. The social stigma associated with nursing seemed unbearable to the Nightingales.

Florence knew better than to argue and decided that she would have to find another way to pursue her interest in nursing. The more involved she became with her patients, the more tempers in the Nightingale household flared. Several years passed. The tension on both sides was tremendous.

Finally, Florence shared her frustration with the Prussian ambassador. He and his wife were interested in improving the conditions of the poor in their country. He told Florence about a very fine institute at Kaiserswerth on the Rhine River in Germany. Begun by Theodor Fliedner and Elizabeth Fry, it had several humanitarian facilities: one was a school to train decent young women to be nurses. Florence now had a course. She knew she belonged at Kaiserswerth, but it would be five long years before her family would finally allow her to go.

Those five years were filled with frustration. When her health began to be affected, Florence traveled to Egypt, France, and Greece. She visited every health-care facility she could find. She took copious notes on care, personnel, procedures, diet, sanitation, buildings, and anything else that affected the patients. Back home in England, she toured every institution for the poor. She carefully organized her findings and analyzed and compiled statistics. The picture they drew was shocking. Florence knew better than anyone the scope of the task that lay before her.

The Nightingales hoped that the strict discipline and spartan regimen of Kaiserswerth would help Florence appreciate her fortunate position and abandon the humiliating course she was pursuing. Indeed, Florence was changed by her experience at Kaiserswerth. Never had she been so happy or content.

She graduated in 1851, at thirty-one years of age, with highest honors. Afterward, when Florence met her sister and mother in Paris, they, too, realized that she had changed, and they bitterly accepted Florence's decision to continue her studies in France. She planned then to return to London to work in a hospital.

In 1853 Florence returned and took a position as manager of the poorly run London Women's Hospital. Finally able to use what she had learned, Florence made many changes. Nothing that caused unnecessary discomfort to her patients or work for her nurses escaped her personal attention. Her nurses were the best she could find in London and were decent, pleasant women. One of the first changes Florence made was political. She battled successfully to allow Catholic and Jewish women admittance to the hospital.

London doctors began to take notice of her work, even if the Nightingales did not. Her family's disapproval troubled Florence, but she blossomed with the challenge of improving and running the women's hospital. One of the visiting doctors was so impressed with the changes Florence had made that he offered her the position of superintendent of nurses at King's College Hospital when its renovation was completed the following year. This offer to a young, beautiful nurse was unprecedented.

In that summer of 1854, reports from the Crimea (a Ukrainian peninsula where the British and French were battling Russian troops) were sent back by the *Times* (London) war correspondent, William Howard Russell. The English reeled from the shock of these reports. Although they were winning on the battlefield, the British forces were losing many lives to cholera and to the neglect of the wounded. William Russell wrote the following (McKown 1966, p. 60):

> The commonest accessories of a hospital are wanting. There is not the least attention paid to decency or clean linen. The stench is appalling. The fetid air can hardly struggle out to taint the atmosphere … and for all I can observe, these men die without the least effort being made to save them…. The sick appear to be tended by the sick, and the dying by the dying. Are there no devoted women amongst us, able and willing to go forth to minister to the sick and suffering soldiers of the East in the hospitals at Scutari? [Now called *Üsküdar*, Scutari, Turkey, was the base for the British forces in the Crimean War.] Are there none of the daughters of England, at this extreme hour of need, ready for such a work of mercy?

Ironically, the letter inspired by such reports that Florence wrote to the British secretary of war, Sir Sidney Herbert, crossed in the mail with his letter to her. Each asked the other to help. Florence was appointed superintendent of the Female Nursing Establishment of the English General Hospitals in Turkey. All England was surprised, and finally even the Nightingales were impressed and lent their support. Florence was given free rein to organize, equip, and manage a nursing expedition to the hospital at Scutari. Within a week's time, Florence selected thirty-eight young women (many of whom were nuns), outfitted them with uniforms, and set sail. Those who did not know Florence marveled that this young woman could organize so grand a venture in seven days. Those who knew her were not at all surprised. "I have been training for this all my life," she wrote in her journal. Florence set off in fall 1854, at age thirty-four, with the blessings of all England. She would need them for what lay ahead in Scutari.

Florence and her nurses found conditions at Scutari worse than Russell had reported in the *Times*. The hospital there was a cesspool of mud and human waste. Half the structure had burned down. In the floor were holes large enough to fall through. Wounded soldiers lay on the floors in the blood-soaked uniforms they had worn into battle. Virtually no supplies were available with which to treat patients or to clean. The menu of half-cooked peas with raw meat never changed. Patients were fortunate to receive water even once a day. These deficiencies, however, were comparatively easy for the nurses to overcome with hard work, determination, and the supplies they had brought with them. It was much more difficult to break down the wall of hostility and resistance that they met from the doctors at Scutari.

Without the doctors' permission, there was nothing the nurses could do but wait, all the while trying not to become dispirited by the anguished screams of the patients. Florence let the doctors know that the nurses would be willing to feed the most critical patients and to share their medical provisions. When the next load of wounded arrived, Florence and her nurses met them outside the hospital with warm, nourishing drinks. The doctors could not refuse this service to their patients. They were grateful when the nurses slipped into the wards during this period of chaos and exhaustion and quietly began to care for the sick and wounded soldiers. In the once hostile doctors, a seed of respect sprouted for these nurses and their work.

With her own money, Florence purchased the supplies that were desperately needed at the hospital. Whatever the doctors or patients required, Florence was somehow able to find. They began to believe that she could perform miracles. Local residents were hired to clean the hospital from top to bottom. The cesspool beneath the structure was drained and rebuilding begun in the burned half of the hospital. Florence set up a laundry to ensure a steady supply of clean linens and shirts. Then she went to see about the supplies that should have been in Scutari.

Florence found most of the supplies rotting in warehouses. The signature of an authorized person was needed to release them. As Florence grew more desperate and angry over these senseless delays, she began to release the supplies herself. She set up a warehouse where the supplies could be distributed quickly and easily. Government officials wailed, but they could not stop her. Florence calmly but firmly informed anyone standing between her and her patients that the rules needed to be changed—then she proceeded to do what could not be done. When insulted, Florence refused to respond. Using her charm, wit, and diplomacy, she managed by coaxing, cajoling, or commanding to secure whatever her patients needed.

When work on the burned wing stopped because of a strike, Florence funded the repairs herself. Miraculously, the wing was ready when the next shipload of wounded arrived. Florence worked twenty-hour days and slept at the hospital on a cot behind a small screen. She wrote letters to each patient's family and met with streams of government officials, officers, doctors, and ministers, making sure that each patient received whatever was needed. An inspiring leader, Florence kept her nurses performing admirably and somehow managed to be wherever she was needed most.

Florence feared no disease and spent hours on her knees caring for the soldiers. She bathed them, wrote and read letters for them, held their hands through surgery, encouraged them to live, and held water to their dying lips. Walking through the wards with a lantern in her hand, Florence spent many long hours of the night in a silent, solitary vigil. One soldier spoke for thousands when he wrote home, "What a comfort it was to see her pass even…. We lay there by hundreds, but we could kiss her shadow as it fell and lay our heads on the pillow again, content" (Cosner 1988, p. 24). These nightly patrols earned Florence the title Lady with the Lamp.

Florence also sent scathing reports to her mentor and friend, Sir Sidney Herbert, complaining about the ineptitude, abuse, and neglect that she had discovered. She suggested several reforms, many of which were enacted immediately. In less than six months, Florence had transformed the hospital into a clean, orderly facility. Death rates fell from 42 to 22 percent.

In England, as reports of the changes she had made filtered back, Florence became second only to Queen Victoria in the hearts of the English. Soldiers whispered her name in the ward with reverence, and the entire country proudly and gratefully hailed Florence Nightingale.

In spring 1855, with the situation under control at Scutari, Florence decided to check out reports that supplies were being wasted and personnel abused in the front-line hospitals. She was met with bouquets and cheering as she rode through one camp, but she found the staff to be rude and hostile.

They clearly resented her presence and refused to heed her suggestions for using money, supplies, and personnel more efficiently. She stayed at the camp for several days, encouraging the ill and wounded until she, too, was felled by the same fever that had infected many of the patients.

For weeks, Florence was not expected to live. The staff and patients at Scutari wept. The queen sent her personal ambassador to report on Florence's condition. All England prayed, and the crisis passed. Strangers on the street stopped one another to share the news of her recovery. Contributions of money were pooled to buy Florence a gift; these donations were the beginning of the Florence Nightingale Fund. Queen Victoria sent Florence a specially designed brooch, and every British family kept a picture or statuette of Florence on its hearth.

In the fall, although still recuperating, Florence kept on working at Scutari. She set up reading and recreation rooms for recovering patients. Singing classes, theatricals, outdoor sports, and chess tournaments were arranged to give the soldiers something constructive to do. Four schools were established for their enrichment. Florence convinced the government to mail home the money that the soldiers saved by participating in these positive pursuits instead of spending it in barrooms.

Florence was not interested in the national celebration being planned for her return. In disguise, she traveled home aboard a French ship and arrived one evening at Lea Hurst quietly and alone. Her grateful country realized that the only two victories in the senseless, bloody war were both due to Florence Nightingale: the image of the British soldier had been elevated from that of a drunken brute to that of a brave, loyal patriot, and nursing had been recognized as an honorable profession.

Florence was too weak to respond to the mail that flooded the household. Parthenope answered Florence's correspondence and protected her privacy. Florence did not stop working, however. She was consumed by the amount of work that remained to be done at home in England. She began to collect more information about the health conditions of the British army. Growing more angry as the evidence of poor conditions mounted, she worked more than she slept. With the help of fiercely loyal friends and family, Florence produced and published a one-thousand-page report within six months. She was a hard taskmaster but demanded more of herself than of anyone.

Florence was finally able to share with Queen Victoria what she had learned at Scutari about the terrible health conditions of the British army. With her characteristic quiet charm and selfless ways and aided by the queen's blessing, Florence won the heart of the new secretary of war. The needed reform of the British army would be ordered, and Florence herself would tell the army what needed to be done. The path was sometimes rocky, but eventually all the changes were made.

Florence also brought about improvements in civilian hospitals. She used the money in the Florence Nightingale Fund to open her first Nightingale Home and School for Training Nurses in 1860. In poor health, Florence spent much of her time working from her bed. She also published *Notes on Nursing,* a classic textbook for nursing students; it was published in three editions. World leaders submitted hospital plans for her approval or asked her to design plans for them. Florence founded the British School for Midwives and responded to President Lincoln's plea for advice about field hospitals for the union troops. She sent several of her graduates into England's poorhouse infirmaries to lead reform there. This action led directly to the formation of the Metropolitan and National Nursing Association in 1875; it was the first association of visiting nurses. In 1872 Jean Henri Dunant founded the International Red Cross but credited Florence with inspiring him by her work in the Crimea.

Florence designed report forms for hospitals (both military and civilian), regularly gathered data, and designed charts so that she could present the information to health officials. Her design, which she called "a cockscomb of biostatistics of life and death" (the antecedent of our modern pie charts), was a powerful tool in bringing about social reform. She is greatly admired as a statistician.

Once the British health-care system was well on its way to reform, Florence began the formidable task of reforming the health-care system in India. From her bed, with the protection and help of her family, Florence was able to accomplish a great deal in India without ever going there. Her understanding of the conditions in India was so complete that anyone planning to visit there first sought her advice.

As the years passed, Florence began to find the peace that had eluded her in her earlier years. Visiting with the nursing students who attended her schools gave her great pleasure. She also enjoyed spending time with close family members and their children but used her illness as a shield to guard against unwanted visitors. She never allowed her illness, however, to stand in the way of establishing needed reforms. She worked relentlessly, driven by the need to make a difference.

In 1901 Florence lost her sight and gradually her other faculties as well. The one who had cared so well for so many needed to be cared for. In 1907 she became the first woman to receive the distinguished Order of Merit from the British government. Shortly afterward, she slipped into a coma. She was not aware of the celebration marking the fiftieth anniversary of the founding of the Nightingale Training School for Nurses in May 1910. At the time there were more than one thousand of these schools in the United States alone.

On 13 August of that year, Florence Nightingale passed quietly to her reward, leaving the world a better place. She had indeed made a difference.

Diana L. Vermeulen
Goshen Middle School
Goshen, Indiana

Suggested Reading

Cosner, Shaaron. *War Nurses*. New York: Walker & Co., 1988.

Kopf, Edwin W. "Florence Nightingale as Statistician." *Journal of the American Statistical Association* 15 (December1916): 388–404.

Leighton, Margaret. *The Story of Florence Nightingale*. New York: Grosset & Dunlap, 1952.

McKown, Robin. *Heroic Nurses*. New York: G. P. Putnam's Sons, 1966.

Elizabeth Blackwell

—First Woman Doctor

You may have heard this riddle:

> A man and his son were riding in a car late at night. While traveling at a high rate of speed, the car left the highway and crashed into a tree. The man and his son were transported to the nearest hospital for emergency medical treatment. As soon as the boy was wheeled into the operating room, the attending physician exclaimed, "I can't operate on this boy; he's my son!" How can this be?

The answer is that the doctor at the hospital is the boy's mother. The riddle assumes that people will not consider the possibility that the physician is a woman.

Women doctors are now common, but to people in the United States in the mid-1800s, the idea was considered preposterous. Women could be nurses or midwives—but never doctors! In those days, "nice" women fainted at the sight of blood, and they certainly would never talk about the workings of the body!

The idea of becoming a doctor was suggested to Elizabeth Blackwell as she held the hand of a dying friend, Mary Donaldson. Mary was suffering from what was probably uterine cancer. The modesty demanded of a Victorian-age woman kept Mary from discussing gynecological problems and symptoms with her male doctor. An earlier treatment may have been prescribed had she been able to consult a female physician. From her deathbed, Mary encouraged Elizabeth to consider becoming a doctor. At first, Elizabeth was shocked at such an idea and declared the suggestion absurd and impossible. But try as she might, Elizabeth could not put the suggestion out of her mind.

Elizabeth Blackwell was born in Bristol, England, on 3 February 1821. She was the third of the nine children born to Hannah and Samuel Blackwell. The success of Samuel's sugar-refinery business allowed the Blackwell family to enjoy a prosperous life. Like the children of most well-to-do British families of this time, the Blackwell children were educated at home. However, unlike most parents, Samuel Blackwell considered the education of his girls to be just as important as that of his boys. He insisted that they all study the same subjects, and he shared his enthusiasm for learning with all his children.

Because of political unrest and decreasing prices in the sugar market, the Blackwell family decided to emigrate to America in 1832 to "make a new start." The family found a house in New York City, and Samuel Blackwell had no trouble setting up a sugar refinery near the city's docks. Although Mr. Blackwell's business prospered, he was troubled that the sugar he refined was grown on plantations in the Caribbean where the labor was provided by slaves.

Mr. Blackwell detested the practice of slavery and soon found himself involved in the antislavery movement. By the fall of 1833, he had become a friend and supporter of William Lloyd Garrison, a fiery leader of the abolitionist movement. The Blackwell family often hosted in their home such antislavery figures as Garrison, Theodore D. Weld, and the Reverend Samuel Cox.

By 1835 the Blackwell family had grown to eleven members, and they decided to move to a larger home with more land. They settled into a new home across the Hudson River in Jersey City, New Jersey. The

Blackwell children were delighted with the surrounding fields and woods and the opportunities for exploration they offered. The children commuted into New York City each day for their formal education; Elizabeth enjoyed this independent lifestyle.

However, life for the Blackwell family changed abruptly a year later when Samuel Blackwell's sugar refinery burned to the ground in the Great Manhattan Fire of 1835. The loss of the refinery was a financial disaster for the Blackwells. Servants were dismissed, and the chores were shared among the children. Elizabeth, who had been practicing the piano for five hours a day, had to give up her music lessons. Her father began reading books on sugar-beet production and experimenting with beet-sugar formulas on the kitchen stove. Two years later, a cousin from Cincinnati, Ohio, convinced Samuel to move his family there and begin a new refinery business.

Cincinnati was a pleasant surprise for the Blackwells. They enjoyed the relaxed city atmosphere as well as the beauty of the rolling hills and the Ohio River. They rented a large house, and Mr. Blackwell established a new refinery near the river. But the optimism about their future waned when Samuel began to run high temperatures and suffer fainting spells. The illness was probably a recurrence of malaria. In August 1838 Samuel Blackwell died while seventeen-year-old Elizabeth held his hand.

Samuel's death left the family with no money and a stack of bills. All the older children needed to work to support the family. The three oldest girls and their aunt decided to open a boarding school. Even though she had little confidence in her abilities, Elizabeth found herself in a teaching position.

During this time, several suitors showed an interest in Elizabeth. She knew that marriage would offer her financial security, but she was also becoming increasingly impatient with the position of women in American society. At the time, everything a woman owned became her husband's property after marriage. A married woman could not sue or be sued in a court of law, appear as a witness, or make a will. These conditions distressed Elizabeth and confirmed her decision to reject marriage.

Instead, Elizabeth continued working at various teaching positions over the next few years. She also attended antislavery meetings, became friends with Harriet Beecher Stowe, and participated in several social clubs. But she soon recognized a personal need to be engaged in some important work. At this point in her life, the suggestion of becoming a doctor was made by her friend Mary Donaldson.

Elizabeth rejected the idea at first, but later she began to contemplate pursuing this vocation. She knew it would take sacrifice, determination, and courage. But she also saw it as a chance to fight a moral battle that would make a lasting difference in society.

Even if Elizabeth had been able to find a medical school that would admit her, the cost of formal medical training was out of the question. She resolved to continue teaching during the day, to earn money, and to study medical books at night. Elizabeth's determination made an impression on a number of associates, and several of them made arrangements for her to borrow medical texts and meet with doctors who could answer her questions.

In 1847 Elizabeth decided to apply to a major medical school. Her letters of application brought a variety of responses: no replies at all, laughter and criticism, words of advice that she abandon her desire, and suggestions to try a European school. After twenty-nine attempts, she was surprised to receive a positive response from Geneva Medical College in upstate New York. The dean of the faculty said in his letter that Blackwell's application had been voted on by the entire student body. What Dean Lee did not mention in his letter was that the students (all male) thought the proposal was a joke and treated it sarcastically with satirical speeches, lively discussions, and finally, the affirmative vote! Miss Blackwell certainly did not treat it as a joke. She arrived on Geneva's campus the night of 6 November and promptly registered as Student 130 the following day.

How did people react to this history-making young woman? Some of the local townspeople stared at her with great curiosity when they saw her on the street. The women were particularly suspicious, concluding that Elizabeth was either a "bad woman" or "insane." Her tireless devotion to her studies, however, earned the respect and admiration of her instructors.

Generally speaking, her classmates were friendly and accepted her presence, even in the anatomy lectures, where the male students made a great effort to stifle embarrassed giggles. In fact, it was noted that the behavior of the male students generally improved whenever Elizabeth was part of the class!

Graduation day at Geneva Medical College in 1849 was like no other before it. Hours before the commencement, the townspeople and guests arrived on the campus. Most noticeable was the number of women present. College President Benjamin Hale began calling the names of the graduates. Because Elizabeth had graduated at the top of her class, her name was called last. The church rang with applause as the diminutive young woman accepted her medical diploma. She blushed and began to leave the stage, then suddenly turned back. Elizabeth addressed the audience: "I thank you. By the help of the Most High, it shall be the effort of my life to shed honor on this diploma." The cheers of her male classmates accompanied her as she took her seat with her fellow physicians.

A woman graduating from medical school was big news. Elizabeth's story quickly appeared in newspapers and magazines in both the United States and Great Britain. Some writers treated the event seriously, but some wrote of it humorously and suggested that she "confine her practice to matters of the heart." As Elizabeth would soon discover, her battle for acceptance as a female physician had just begun.

After graduation Elizabeth returned to Philadelphia, where she had lived before entering Geneva Medical College. She was greeted politely by the medical community, but no one would give her a job. She decided that Paris, then a place of advanced medical activity, was the best place to further her medical career. On her journey, Elizabeth stopped in England for a few weeks to visit her native land. Like any other tourist, she enjoyed visiting many castles and monuments, but she was quite surprised at the celebrity status she was accorded in British hospitals.

Armed with a formal letter of introduction from an American doctor, Elizabeth arrived in Paris and immediately sought out Pierre Louis, a prominent French physician. The distinguished doctor listened as she explained her desire to work in a Paris hospital under the supervision of experienced physicians and to become a surgeon. When she had finished, Pierre Louis coldly advised her to apply to La Maternité, a women's medical center where she could be trained as a midwife. Similar rejections came from other Paris doctors—although one suggested that she could attend lectures disguised as a man! Elizabeth finally decided to spend three months learning obstetrics at La Maternité, the only Paris hospital that would accept her.

At La Maternité, she followed a grueling schedule, as did her classmates, all young French women with no previous medical training. The women worked on twelve-hour day or night shifts, which combined feeding and bathing the patients, assisting the supervising doctors, and attending lectures. Because of her dedication, Elizabeth postponed her goal of becoming a surgeon in order to sign up for another three-month stint at La Maternité. That decision changed her life.

While cleaning the badly infected eye of an infant, Elizabeth accidentally splashed a drop of water into her own eye. When she was unable to open it the following morning, she reported to the infirmary. The news was bad: she had contracted the disease for which she had been treating the baby.

Treatment and bandages were applied for the next three weeks, but the measures were ineffectual. Elizabeth had lost the sight in her left eye, as well as her dream of becoming the first female surgeon. Six months later, the affected eye became inflamed and had to be removed. After a surgeon replaced it with a glass eye, Elizabeth resumed her quest for further medical training.

A cousin in London assisted Elizabeth in obtaining permission to study at Saint Bartholemew, a large London hospital. There she finally found the acceptance and encouragement she had been seeking. Every department of study was open to her! Equally important during this year of study were the people she met. She became friends with Barbara Leigh Smith, a wealthy young intellectual who later became a prominent leader in the British feminist movement. Barbara Smith introduced Elizabeth to Florence Nightingale, a discontented, socially prominent young woman who dreamed of a career in public health, even though her family forbade it. The two women spent hours together discussing medical reform and dreamed of opening a hospital where they could put their ideas into practice.

On finishing her successful year of study at Saint Bartholemew Hospital, Elizabeth Blackwell was eager to return to the United States to begin her own medical practice. She was particularly excited to see her sister Emily, who, inspired by Elizabeth's ground-breaking accomplishments, was enrolled in medical school herself. Elizabeth was not prepared, however, for the hostility and rejection that awaited her in New York. Landlords everywhere were unwilling to rent her space for her office because at the time, a female doctor was suspected of being an abortionist. One landlady finally agreed to rent her space at an outrageous price and complained constantly about Elizabeth's presence.

The harassment continued. Insults were hurled at her in public, and women often crossed the street to avoid her. Her mail frequently contained threatening and obscene remarks. Once again, Elizabeth Blackwell's firm determination took over as she decorated her new office and waited for patients—patients who never came. Faced with empty hours and a vacant room, Elizabeth wrote a series of lectures on physical education for girls. Although these lectures about the female anatomy and the importance of proper diet and exercise would not be considered outstanding today, the information intrigued Elizabeth's small audience. Her listeners spread the word about her approach to preventing female diseases, and she soon found her office occupied by a few loyal patients.

Elizabeth was not making enough money to live on, so she applied for acceptance on the staff at several hospitals. All her applications were refused. By this time, she had become so concerned about the health needs of poor, inner-city residents that she borrowed money from her friends to open a clinic in the slums of Lower Manhattan. The New York Dispensary for Poor Women and Children was crowded with patients on each of the three afternoons a week it was open. Elizabeth treated these people, many of whom had never before seen a doctor, in the clinic as well as in their tenement rooms. The work was draining and never ending.

Emily Blackwell came to help her sister for several months before sailing for Europe to continue her medical studies. Assistance also came from Marie Zakrzewska, a German-born Polish woman who came to America to continue her medical studies. Marie Zakrzewska spoke little English, but Elizabeth knew enough German to communicate with her. Marie agreed to act as Elizabeth's assistant until Elizabeth could teach her English and help her get into medical school. For five months the two worked together as teacher and student—and as friends.

When Marie left to be formally enrolled in medical school, Elizabeth was overcome by loneliness. She adopted a seven-year-old, Irish-born girl named Kitty, whom orphanage workers described as "stupid" and "not very pretty." Elizabeth discovered that Kitty was not stupid at all. Under the same type of education Elizabeth had received as a child, Kitty blossomed and developed to the point of being able to handle the financial accounts for "Doctor," the name Kitty always called her adoptive mother.

At age thirty-five, Elizabeth finally saw one of her dreams come true. After the return of her sister Emily and their friend Marie Zakrzewska, who had recently graduated from medical school, the three women began an intensive fund-raising campaign. What was their goal? They wanted to raise enough money to open a hospital run by women for women. Their tireless efforts raised almost five thousand dollars. With the help of supportive friends and donated materials, the New York Infirmary for Indigent Women and Children formally opened on 12 May 1857. Despite earlier protests and objections from officials throughout the city, the dedication was attended by a large crowd of supporters, including notable leaders in the antislavery and woman-suffrage movements.

Because the hospital charged its patients only four dollars each week—and did not charge if they could not afford it—the hospital was always in financial need. Elizabeth Blackwell's British friends had been urging her to return to England to aid in British women's advancement in the medical field. When friends pointed out that she could raise funds for her hospital by giving lectures, she was persuaded to leave the workings of the hospital in the capable hands of her sister and Marie and travel to England.

Elizabeth Blackwell gave numerous speeches throughout England. She insisted that women must understand the principles of health and the workings of the human body. She challenged women to consider how the field of medicine might benefit from their skills and unique feminine perspective and encouraged them to be more than mere imitators of men. Her lectures met with some contempt but were immensely popular among young women eager to enter the medical profession. Many prominent people, including her old friend Florence Nightingale, urged her to stay in England. However, her return to the United States became imperative when she learned that Marie Zakrzewska had accepted a job as professor of obstetrics at a Boston college. When Elizabeth returned to the United States, she brought with her a large sum of cash and a zeal to return to her work—work that "had a soul!"

The infirmary had prospered in her absence. With the additional funds Elizabeth had raised in England, the hospital's board of trustees purchased a larger and permanent site for the hospital. In 1861 Elizabeth began to campaign for her next goal, a medical school for women. But that goal was postponed by a much greater task: preserving the United States of America.

For the next four years, Elizabeth divided her time between running the hospital and training nurses to aid the Union soldiers wounded in the Civil War. She was in charge of supervising thousands of young women (many of whom had been inspired by Florence Nightingale) who had volunteered to serve under the most wretched conditions.

In April 1865, the Confederacy surrendered to the Union. Elizabeth was then able to devote her energy to expanding the work of the hospital. She was convinced of the importance of sanitary conditions in preventing diseases and was eager to improve people's understanding of basic health conditions. With a supporter's donation, she employed several health inspectors, who went into the slums, bringing soap, disinfectants, and information on health care.

Another of Elizabeth Blackwell's dreams came true on 2 November 1868, when she presided over the opening of the Women's Medical College of the New York Infirmary. This women's college broke new ground. It established demanding entrance requirements, required three years of classroom training instead of ten months, and made other improvements in the training of doctors. Emily Blackwell proved skillful at running both the college and the hospital. This allowed Elizabeth to respond once again to the appeal from her British friends. "Come to England," said one letter. "We need you desperately. Come and help us do for the women of England what you have done for the women of America." What else could an energetic, forty-eight-year-old pioneer who always needed new frontiers to cross do but say yes?

Elizabeth said her main purpose in going to England was to assist other female physicians, but as often happened in her life, she managed to accomplish much more. She found herself lecturing on health and sanitation, family planning, sex education, hazardous work conditions, and other issues that supported her motto, "Prevention is better than cure." Although not everyone agreed with her ideas, she was respected because she was able to chip away gradually at the British medical profession's opposition to female physicians.

Soon after her fifty-eighth birthday in 1879, Elizabeth and Kitty moved into a British seaside cottage, where they lived for the next thirty years. Here Elizabeth wrote books, planned reform campaigns, and entertained friends and colleagues. At the urging of her daughter, Elizabeth used her letters and diary entries to write her autobiography. She gave up her private practice in 1894 but continued to write and speak in behalf of her favorite causes. In 1907 she suffered a fall down a flight of stairs and never fully recovered her alertness and vigor. With Kitty at her side, Elizabeth Blackwell died peacefully on 31 May 1910 at the age of eighty-nine.

What would be a fitting tribute to this great woman? The monument on Elizabeth's grave reads, "The first woman of modern times to graduate in medicine (1849) and the first to be placed on the British Medical Register (1859)." The *Times* (London) summed up her life in this way: "She was in the fullest sense of the word a pioneer." Most people will remember her simply as "the first woman doctor."

Recall the riddle at the beginning of this story. Elizabeth Blackwell changed the way people *think*. She changed the way people think about medicine, public health, preventive medicine, and, of course, the role of women in medicine. Thanks to her pioneering efforts, in 1985—seventy-five years after her death—the American Medical Association listed 80 725 female physicians as members.

When a person has changed the way people think, she has changed the world. Her influence on modern medicine is a fitting tribute to Elizabeth Blackwell.

Caryn Ellison
Twin Branch Elementary School
Mishawaka, Indiana

Suggested Reading

Brown, Jordan. *Elizabeth Blackwell.* New York: Chelsea House, 1989.

Gersh, Harry. *Women Who Made America Great.* Philadelphia: J. B. Lippincott Co., 1962.

Grant, Matthew. *Elizabeth Blackwell, Pioneer Doctor.* Mankato, Minn.: Creative Education, 1974.

Elizabeth Garrett Anderson

—First British Woman Doctor

"My daughter is not going to listen to a freak from America."
"Papa, Miss Blackwell is not a freak; she is a doctor."
"Same thing; no decent woman would do that."

So began Elizabeth Garrett's journey to become England's first female doctor. At twenty-three, she was convinced that life had more to offer than getting dressed up and attending teas. The year was 1859, and women were beginning to seek a place in the world. Before this time, women had been employed only as companions and governesses. Florence Nightingale, however, had recently made nursing an acceptable, even admirable, profession for women. Society had begun to accept the notion that women could make contributions in nonconventional ways.

Newson Garrett looked fondly at his second child. He had risen in the world. His daughter would never need to work. He and his wife, the former Louisa Dunnell, had begun as pawnbrokers in a very rough London district. Within four years Mr. Garrett had expanded this business, moved to a larger shop, and become a silversmith. Each succeeding year had brought more financial success and another baby to the growing family. By 1841 Newson Garrett had settled his family in a large Georgian home in Aldeburgh.

Most children from middle-class families were confined to nurseries, but Elizabeth and her older sister, Louisa, were allowed to explore. They wandered marshes, beaches, and the docks where the fishermen moored their boats. Although their brothers had a tutor, Elizabeth and her sister learned their first lessons from their mother. By the time Elizabeth was ten, her parents had eight children, and her mother could not carry out all her responsibilities alone. The Garretts hired a governess to supervise and teach Louisa and Elizabeth.

Elizabeth detested the regimented life imposed by her governess. And the governess could not cope with Elizabeth's inquisitive mind. Their daily lessons turned into a battleground. Three years later Mr. Garrett decided to send his daughters to the Boarding School for Ladies at Blackheath. Although Elizabeth was not taught science or mathematics, she learned to write well. While at the school, she also developed an appreciation for books. By 1851 she and her sister had completed their schooling and returned home. For the next nine years, Elizabeth was a dutiful daughter. She continued to read and study Latin during this time. She also enjoyed the pleasures of the countryside: picnics, parties, riding, skating, sailing, visiting friends, and so forth.

In 1859 Elizabeth and her best friend, Emily Davies, wanted to attend the guest lectures given by Elizabeth Blackwell, who had earned a medical degree from an American college. Dr. Blackwell was the first woman to have become a medical doctor in modern times. Elizabeth's father believed that Dr. Blackwell must be a freak, since no "nice" woman would want to do what doctors did. Elizabeth coaxed her father into having one of his business partners check out "this Blackwell woman." Her father's partner reported favorably on Dr. Blackwell and even gave Mr. Garrett a letter of introduction for Elizabeth.

Ecstatic, Elizabeth arrived in London a day early, but her visit with Dr. Blackwell was somewhat disconcerting. Not that the kind doctor was intimidating, but Dr. Blackwell had assumed that Elizabeth Garrett had requested the meeting because she, too, wanted to study medicine. This assumption startled Elizabeth. She had not felt particularly drawn to medicine. She sensed only that her life lacked purpose. After her talk with Dr. Blackwell, Elizabeth attended all three lectures with even greater interest. Could she really become a doctor? She had never thought of the possibility.

Elizabeth and Emily often had serious conversations. One afternoon they were discussing the plight of women. They decided that the only way to improve the lives of women was to improve the education of women.

"I shall open the universities to women," declared Emily, "and you shall tackle the field of medicine."

"What will Papa say?" Elizabeth replied, although she already knew what his response would be.

"Absolutely not," declared Mr. Garrett. "The idea of a woman doctor is repulsive."

"But, Papa, everyone admired Florence Nightingale and her nursing work in the war, including you."

"That was not doctoring, and she was not my daughter."

Mrs. Garrett's response was also predictable. She cried and threatened to die of disgrace.

Elizabeth was a quiet, gracious, and committed young woman. But these qualities did not diminish her determination. Once she had decided to walk a certain road, she would not be deterred. Eventually her father gave his consent to Elizabeth's studying medicine but declared that he would never approve of the disgusting idea. Even so, he accompanied his daughter when she went to seek the best medical minds in London. When told that she would never be placed on the British Medical Register or even admitted to any of the universities, Elizabeth started to become discouraged.

Surprisingly, her father became angry. His daughter had had a better-than-average education, and he knew she could do anything she set her mind to. On one occasion when Elizabeth was asked why she did not simply become a nurse instead of a doctor, she responded, "I prefer to earn a thousand rather than twenty pounds a year." This occasion was one of the few times Elizabeth lost her temper in the face of discouragement and ridicule.

Besides women doctors' being virtually unheard of at this time, Elizabeth had trouble being taken seriously for another reason. She was petite and pretty, and no one believed that she would finish medical training before she married. Elizabeth decided to test her commitment to medicine by spending a trial period as a nurse in a surgical ward at Middlesex Hospital. At first, the other nurses did not trust her. They thought that being a "lady," she might put on airs, but eventually her graciousness and tact won them over.

The chief resident physician at Middlesex Hospital and the dean of the affiliated medical school were particularly impressed with Elizabeth and arranged for her to attend operations and to follow medical students on rounds. Soon she was spending so much time with the students that she offered to pay the same fees that they did. The treasurer refused her offer, however, because accepting a fee would be equivalent to recognizing Elizabeth as a medical student. Since she was not allowed to attend the medical lectures, she engaged tutors. Proper conduct required that the lessons be held in the home of her married sister. Gradually Elizabeth managed to attend some of the medical lectures by politely approaching the professors and tactfully asking their permission to sit in. In every class in which Elizabeth participated, she won a certificate of honor, but she was told to keep the awards secret.

One day a visiting physician was questioning the students as they went about their rounds. He asked a question about a case and waited quite a while but received no response. Normally, Elizabeth would stand back and just listen. This time, however, after waiting for the male students to reply, Elizabeth quietly gave the correct answer. The physician thanked her and laughed. The men were so embarrassed and outraged that they circulated a petition to dismiss her. A few of the students started a petition to keep her, but they were in the minority.

Elizabeth and her father decided to test the universities' adherence to their previous decisions. The universities had said that they would never graduate her with a medical degree. Elizabeth thought it would be useless to study if she was forbidden to practice medicine. She and her father searched for a loophole and found one. The Licentiate of the Society of Apothecaries (L.S.A.) entitled holders of the degree to practice medicine. The charter of the Society of Apothecaries stated that "all persons" desirous of obtaining this degree had to complete the required courses. Elizabeth was a "person." To qualify, she had to be apprenticed to a licensed physician for five years and attend a certain number of required lecture courses. All persons who fulfilled these requirements would be allowed to take the licensing examinations. The apothecaries admitted that they would have to let her take the examinations if she met these conditions and told her to come back in five years. They were certain that she would marry long before then.

Elizabeth became apprenticed to Dr. Plaskitt at Saint Andrews University in Scotland. There she began the slow process of collecting the various certificates for the required courses. On 29 October 1862, a clerk made an error and accidentally let her pay for a course that a professor had permitted her to attend. The authorities begged her to return the ticket and said they would give her a refund. Her father threatened a lawsuit. On this occasion, the male student body was on her side. However, Elizabeth tactfully arranged to finish the course privately with the sympathetic professor. After six years, she had met the necessary requirements to take the licensing examinations.

When she came before the Society of Apothecaries, the members were shocked. They had never expected to see Elizabeth again, and they refused to let her take the examinations. Again her father came to the rescue and threatened to sue. Realizing that it would lose the suit, the Society of Apothecaries permitted Elizabeth to take the examinations in

September 1865. Of the seven candidates, Elizabeth qualified first. The examinations were easy for her, and in 1866 Elizabeth Garrett, L.S.A., was listed in the British Medical Register. She was twenty-nine years old.

After this incident, the Society of Apothecaries wrote a new charter that barred women. Elizabeth Blackwell, who had a foreign degree, and Elizabeth Garrett were the only female members of the society. Twelve years later, an act of Parliament was required to admit women to the medical register.

After becoming a member of the Society of Apothecaries, Elizabeth opened a small clinic, Saint Mary's Dispensary for Women, in a slum in London. Years later it became the New Hospital for Women. Elizabeth loved her work among the poor. In her spare time she worked for women's voting rights.

In 1868 Elizabeth learned that the University of Paris had opened its doors to women. She immediately contacted her ambassador to make arrangements to take the medical examinations. Elizabeth not only had to review all her past course work but also had to learn to convey her medical knowledge in French. Over a two-year period, she took several examinations and submitted a thesis on migraines. She passed and became a licensed medical doctor.

Elizabeth longed for a position in a regular hospital. In February 1870 she applied for a job at Shadwell Hospital for Children, but one of the board members, James Skelton Anderson, was determined to keep her off the staff. Mr. Anderson was a handsome, wealthy bachelor. On meeting Dr. Garrett, he dropped his objections. Elizabeth assumed the vacant position on the staff. She also found many opportunities to talk with, and write to, Mr. Anderson.

Elizabeth became interested in politics, and she ran for the local school board. The husbands and fathers of her patients wanted someone they knew and trusted on the board. She was elected by an overwhelming majority. While on the school board, she voted that only females be allowed to teach infant and senior girls, thus opening up the teaching profession to hundreds of women. She also insisted that children require light, fresh air, bathrooms, and space to play.

James Anderson had come to admire Elizabeth's boundless energy. He proposed marriage, and she accepted. Unexpected reactions to the engagement came from many quarters. Many of Elizabeth's friends were angry or saddened. They were afraid that she would give up everything: her job, her position on the school board, and her voice for women's rights. Even Elizabeth's father was disappointed. He did not want her to waste the time and money she had spent to become a doctor. Her father relented when James assured Mr. Garrett that he would not interfere with his wife's career. Elizabeth worked right up to the eve of her wedding. On 9 February 1871, Elizabeth and James were married in a very small ceremony at the unusual hour of 8:30 A.M.

James became his wife's most courageous supporter. On one occasion, one of Elizabeth's patients required a risky operation, but the New Hospital for Women refused to let its founder operate. Because of the high risk of mortality, many London teaching hospitals prohibited this surgery. The patient seemed certain to die, and the hospital feared that it would be held responsible for letting a woman perform surgery. James leased a house and had a room in it scrubbed, whitewashed, and completely furnished as an operating room. He also hired a private nurse. Elizabeth successfully performed the surgery, and the patient recovered.

Elizabeth Garrett Anderson was one of the first women to successfully combine a professional career and family life. On 28 July 1873, her daughter, Louisa Garrett Anderson, was born. Four years later Elizabeth gave birth to a son, Alan Garrett Anderson. Louisa also became a doctor, serving as chief surgeon in a military hospital.

During her lifetime, Elizabeth made many contributions to society. Among other achievements, she served for twenty years as dean of the London School of Medicine for Women. When she and her husband retired, James was elected mayor of Aldeburgh, and after his death, the city asked Elizabeth to finish his term of office. She accepted and immediately began plans for several building projects. After the next election, she returned to office as the first woman ever to be elected mayor of a city in England. Elizabeth died in 1917. The hospital she founded—the Elizabeth Garrett Anderson Hospital—now bears her name in honor of her great contribution to the field of medicine.

Jaci Pokorny Byrne
Saint Anthony de Padua School
South Bend, Indiana

Suggested Reading

Hume, Ruth Fox. *Great Women of Medicine*. New York: Random House, 1964.

Lovejoy, Esther Pohl. *Women Doctors of the World*. New York: Macmillan Co., 1957.

Lutzker, Edythe. *Women Gain a Place in Medicine*. New York: McGraw-Hill Book Co., 1969.

Manton, Jo. *Elizabeth Garrett Anderson*. New York: E. P. Dutton & Co., 1965.

O'Neill, Lois Decker. *The Women's Book of World Records and Achievements*. New York: DaCapo Press, 1979.

Marie Sklodowska Curie

—Recipient of Two Nobel Prizes

Life is not easy for any of us. But what of that? We must have perseverance and above all confidence in ourselves. We must believe that we are gifted for something, and that this thing, at whatever cost, must be attained.

—Marie Curie

Marie and Pierre Curie returned to the site of their long day of work to enjoy the bluish glow of the newly discovered chemical element radium. This shared moment of wonder was the conclusion of forty-five months of strenuous physical and mental labor to isolate the element the scientific world had not even imagined. Marie was to "remember forever this evening of glowworms, this magic" (Curie 1938, pp. 176–77).

The girl who grew up to become one of the most important scientists of modern times was born in Warsaw, Poland, in 1867. Later in life she would be called Marie Curie, but her birth name was Marja Sklodowska. (In Polish, last names end with an *a* for females and an *i* for males.) Her father, Wladislaw Sklodowski, was university educated and taught mathematics and physics at several different high schools in Warsaw. Bronislawa Boguska Sklodowska, Marja's mother, had received a good education at a private girls' school in Warsaw. She decided to become a teacher at the same school and eventually became the school's director.

Seven months after Marja's birth, her father accepted a new high school position that required him to live at the school. Marja's mother left her position at the girls' school to take care of her five children in their new home.

As is traditional in Poland, all five Sklodowski children were called by nicknames. The oldest daughter, Sophie, was always "Zosia"; Joseph was called "Jozio"; Bronislawa became "Bronya"; Helen was "Hela"; and the youngest, Marja, was addressed by many affectionate names, most commonly "Manya." Young Manya had ash-gray eyes, and her curly, blond hair was always out of control.

As a little girl, Manya was fascinated by the objects in a glass case in her father's study. Professor Sklodowski had used the glass tubes, scientific scale, electroscope, and mineral samples in his classroom. On tiptoes, Manya marveled at the strange "physics apparatus," unaware that she would later use these instruments when she became a scientist.

Manya was a bright student, two years younger than her classmates. She attended a private girls' school where she was secretly taught Polish history in the Polish language, a double crime according to the authorities who represented Russia, which occupied Poland at the time. Manya had strong nationalistic feelings even though her country no longer officially existed.

Because Professor Sklodowski was not submissive enough to the Russian educational administration, he was demoted in 1873 and lost his school housing. After moving to an apartment, the Sklodowskis had to take in boarders to make ends meet. Also, in an attempt to pay for the treatment of his wife's tuberculosis, which she had contracted before Manya's birth, Professor Sklodowski made an unsuccessful investment in a steam mill and lost his savings of thirty thousand rubles. He long regretted this gamble, which brought poverty to him and his family.

Manya's oldest sister, Zosia, contracted typhus from one of the boarders and died in 1876. Madame Sklodowska died in 1878, leaving Professor Sklodowski with four young children and no savings. These childhood experiences may explain some of Manya's adult behavior. Because of her illness, Manya's mother was unable to give her the physical affection so necessary to a child's development. Since tuberculosis is extremely contagious, Manya was never kissed by her mother. As a result, Manya found it difficult to relate to people on a personal level. And because of her family's financial struggles, Manya never changed her preference for a simple and thrifty lifestyle.

During her high school years, Manya attended a "gymnasium," a government-controlled Russian school with Germanic discipline and traditions. The school tried unsuccessfully to control both her loyalty and her curly hair. In 1883 at the end of her secondary school studies at the gymnasium, Manya was awarded a gold medal for being the top student. She followed in the tradition of her brother Joseph and her sister Bronya, who had both been gold-medal winners. These accomplishments made their father very proud.

The next year, Manya's father encouraged her to take a year off and spend time with different relatives in the country before she chose her livelihood. She happily gave up her school books for attending dances, seeing the countryside, enjoying life, and having fun. During one particular party, Manya danced so much that she wore through the soles of a new pair of russet leather shoes. During that year, she wrote to a schoolmate, "I can't believe geometry or algebra ever existed; I have completely forgotten them."

To help improve the Sklodowski family's finances, the children began to give private lessons in mathematics and foreign languages—with little reward. Manya and Bronya became involved in the "floating university." This informal group of young intellectuals met in homes to learn and discuss ideas. They were always under the threat of arrest by police because education and thought were strictly controlled by the Russian occupiers.

Since a university education was not available to women in Poland, Bronya dreamed of going to Paris to study medicine. Manya dreamed of traveling to the University of Paris, the Sorbonne, to be trained as a teacher so she could teach in her beloved Poland. Bronya had saved enough money to pay for one of the five years of study necessary to become a doctor. Manya proposed that Bronya go to Paris the next year. While Bronya was going to school, Manya would get a job as a governess and send her money. After Bronya became a doctor, she could finance Manya's schooling in Paris.

Manya endured five years as a governess for several different families. She sent most of her salary to help Bronya and her aging father. Unfortunately, her employers taught Manya that great kindness or intelligence does not necessarily go along with great wealth. Isolated in remote rural areas, she at times lost her ambition to go to Paris. At one of her posts, she fell in love with her employer's college-aged son. Since she was poor, the family thought she was an unsuitable match for the young man, and he lacked the strength to defy his parents.

After three years in Paris, Bronya was doing well in medical school; she had found a job and had made plans to marry a Polish medical student, Casimir Dluski. Bronya instructed Professor Sklodowski not to send her any more money and to begin to save for Manya's education. Manya, however, was no longer sure she wanted to go to Paris. She had been deeply hurt by her unsuccessful romance, and she doubted her academic abilities. Again working as a private tutor, Manya spent the next year at home with her father in Warsaw, associating with young intellectuals and conducting science experiments. In the laboratory, Manya finally found her place in the world.

Manya arrived in Paris in 1891 at the age of twenty-four. She changed her first name to Marie and enrolled in the Sorbonne. In her first classes, she discovered that she did not know French well enough to understand her professors' rapid speech. She also realized that she had major gaps in her mathematics and science education. Marie worked diligently to catch up.

After living for a time with Bronya and her lively family, Marie moved into a quieter apartment closer to the Sorbonne. To save money, she often did without heat in the winter and would use the university library as much as possible at night because it had light and heat. Marie continued to wear the out-of-style, worn-out dresses she had brought from Warsaw, and she lived for weeks at a time on just bread and butter with tea. Fortunately, Bronya and Casimir occasionally took Marie to their apartment for a few days of food and rest.

Marie fell in love with the atmosphere of the laboratory. In 1893 she graduated at the top of her class with a master's degree in physics. Her savings were gone, but she received the Alexandrovitch Scholarship, which enabled her to continue her education outside Poland. Marie had dreamed of returning to the Sorbonne to obtain a second master's degree—in mathematics. Marie earned this degree in 1894, testing second highest in her class.

At the beginning of 1894, Marie met Pierre Curie. Pierre was a thirty-four-year-old, established physicist teaching at the School of Physics, Chemistry, and Natural Science (P.C.N.), a less prestigious undergraduate school associated with the Sorbonne. Pierre and his brother Jacques had invented a device that precisely measures small quantities of electricity. Marie used this apparatus in later research. Pierre's specialty was the study of crystal structures. He had invented the Curie scale and formulated Curie's law, which deals with magnetism and temperature.

Marie's knowledge and devotion to experimental science immediately captivated Pierre. He wrote many letters to her after she returned that summer to Poland. He had already asked her to marry him, but Marie did not want to leave her beloved Poland permanently. Finally, Pierre convinced her to return for another year of study at the Sorbonne. They envisioned working side by side in the laboratory. The couple married in 1895.

In their early years of marriage, Marie and Pierre enjoyed escaping to the countryside to ride their bicycles. Pierre loved to take nature walks. He did his best thinking in quiet natural surroundings. One amusing story paints the picture of a very intelligent but absent-minded professor: One day the Curies' cook asked Pierre what he thought of the steak she had prepared. Pierre is said to have answered, "Did I eat a beefsteak? It's quite possible."

In a letter to her sister Bronya, Marie described Pierre as "the best husband one could dream of…. He is a true gift of heaven, and the more we live together the more we love each other." Marie and Pierre relied heavily on each other, both professionally and emotionally. Their daughter Eve later described Pierre as tranquil and a daydreamer and Marie as zealous and down to earth.

The Curies lived simply. Their first home had only a table and two chairs in the living room. The meager furnishings were easy to keep clean and did not encourage visitors.

Marie and Pierre's first child, Irène, was born in 1897. Marie was soon back in the laboratory. To complete her doctorate, she was required to do original research. Pierre, as an experienced scientist, was her guide.

Wilhelm Roentgen had discovered X rays, the next shorter band of electromagnetic radiation than ultraviolet, in 1895. Henri Becquerel then discovered in salt compounds of uranium what Marie Curie later named radioactivity. The nature and source of this radiation energy became the topic for Marie's doctoral thesis.

With Pierre's help, Marie secured a small storeroom at the P.C.N. for her laboratory. She used two of Pierre's inventions—a Curie electrometer and a piezoelectric quartz—to measure the ability of the radiation to cause an electrical discharge. Marie questioned whether elements other than uranium were radioactive. She found that one other known element, thorium, also emitted rays of similar intensity. She then tested almost eighty other mineral samples. She was surprised when three samples—pitchblende, chalcocite, and uranite—were four times as radioactive as expected. Marie hypothesized that some unknown element must have even stronger radioactivity than uranium or thorium.

In 1898 Pierre decided to join in Marie's research and abandon his study of crystals. They worked side by side in the damp storeroom, enjoying their common passion for research. They separated by chemical processes all the components of the pitchblende ore. They discarded the nonradioactive ones and continued to process and further separate the remaining radioactive parts. Instead of finding one new radioactive element, Marie and Pierre isolated two strongly radioactive elements. They named them *polonium*, in honor of Marie's homeland, and *radium*.

Because the discovery of these two new elements upset long-standing theories about the composition of matter, the scientific community required proof of their existence. Pierre and Marie had first thought that the new elements might constitute as much as 1 percent of the pitchblende ore. The elements, however, were much more radioactive than they had believed: they constituted closer to one-millionth of 1 percent of the ore.

The Curies needed three things to enable them to continue their research: (1) an enormous supply of pitchblende ore, (2) a laboratory and a place to process the ore, and (3) money to pay for the work. The Curies could receive tons of residue from pitchblende ore from mines in Bohemia, but they needed to pay for the shipping. The P.C.N. gave Pierre the use of an abandoned shed with a leaky skylight, inadequate heat and ventilation, and a dirt floor.

The Curies had no financial resources except their earnings. Pierre's teaching at P.C.N. paid little and took time away from his research. But he took on extra teaching chores to help pay their expenses. Marie had not received a salary for her research. In 1900 she finally obtained a teaching position. Because she was a woman, she was not allowed to teach at a French university; instead, she taught at the Normal School at Sèvres, a two-year teacher-training school.

Marie and Pierre toiled from 1898 through 1902 to isolate one-tenth of a gram of radium salts and to estimate that its atomic mass is 225. Delays were caused by contamination of the samples in the poor conditions in the shed, by the need for Marie and Pierre to spend time in teaching, and by accidents caused by Marie's inexperience. Pierre became discouraged, but Marie encouraged him to press on.

Pierre focused on the properties of radium while Marie worked to isolate the pure radium salts. Marie's job was more physically demanding. She had to carry and lift the ore into a great kettle. She then stirred and poured off the liquids for hours at a time while smoke stung her eyes and throat. The process was repeated, kettle after kettle and day after day.

Twenty years after her graduation from high school, Marie completed her doctoral examination and defended her thesis. Pierre and Marie declined the opportunity to patent radium and its manufacture. Marie thought that it was "contrary to the scientific spirit" to profit from their discovery. But Marie and Pierre answered the questions of other scientists and would-be refiners of radium. In the early 1900s, radium sold for 750 000 gold francs, the equivalent of $150 000 a gram. (There are 31 grams in one ounce.) Commercially produced radium was reserved for scientific research and for the treatment of cancer by "Curietherapy." Curietherapy used radium to partially burn the outer layer of the skin, destroying the cancer.

Marie was deeply saddened by the death of her father in 1902, and she was working too many hours without enough food or rest. She miscarried in 1903, but after some forced rest, she successfully bore a second daughter, Eve, in 1904. The difficult pregnancy and the demands of her work left her very weak. Pierre's poor health left him unable to work much. Although diagnosed as rheumatism, his condition was probably related to his exposure to radiation.

In 1903 Pierre and Marie were honored—along with Henri Becquerel—with a Nobel Prize in physics for their collective discoveries in radioactivity. At that time, Marie was the first and only celebrated woman scientist. Early in 1904, she shared the French Osiris Prize with Edouard Branly. The prizes brought the Curies both fame and much-needed money to continue their research. They tried to avoid the public acclamation, since it distracted them from their research, and they continued to live frugally.

Pierre had long desired to have an adequately financed laboratory. In 1904 he was finally made a professor at the Sorbonne and given a small laboratory staffed by three assistants. Marie became the chief of laboratory work. Finally, Marie had a salary and official status in the laboratory, and the Curies had the resources to continue their research. Then tragedy struck.

In 1906 Pierre Curie was killed while walking down the middle of a narrow road on a rainy day. A horse-drawn wagon knocked him down, and the rear wheels crushed his head. Mourning his absent-minded son, Dr. Eugène Curie asked sadly, "What was he dreaming of this time?" Marie suffered greatly at the loss of her beloved husband and partner in research.

A month later, Marie Curie, at thirty-eight, was offered Pierre's teaching and research position at the Sorbonne. She was the first woman offered a teaching position in a French university. Two years later, she was promoted to professor.

Pierre's father had lived with Marie and Pierre for several years. After Pierre's death, Dr. Curie provided emotional support for Marie and help with young Eve and Irène until his own death in 1910. Dr. Curie had a strong influence on Irène's interest in science. Irène later followed her mother into the study of radioactivity.

Marie wanted her children to be hardy and physically active. She passed on to them a spirit of independence, a love of outdoor activities, an energy for work, and a disinterest in money.

Marie's achievements were not recognized by most French scientists because of their professional envy and because she was a woman. She was never admitted to the French Academy of Science. Her work was, however, recognized outside of France, and she was awarded another Nobel Prize in 1911 for her preparation of one gram of pure radium. She had earlier isolated radium salts as compounds with chlorides or bromides and discovered a new method of measuring the radioactivity of substances. Marie's 1903 prize in physics had been the first awarded to a woman. She is one of only two people to have won two Nobel Prizes in physics, medicine, or chemistry and one of only eight women to have won the prize in those sciences.

By 1905 the political climate had changed in Poland, permitting greater intellectual freedom. In 1912, Marie was invited to Warsaw to head a yet-to-be-established laboratory of radioactivity. But she declined the offer that would have allowed her to escape the gossip and occasional ridicule she endured in France. Marie feared that if she left France, the promise made by the Sorbonne and the Pasteur Institute of a large, new laboratory of radioactivity—the Institute of Radium—would be withdrawn.

Marie took a personal interest in the design and construction of the Paris laboratory and its adjoining facility, where the research would be applied to medicine. The Institute of Radium was completed in July 1914; however, the beginning of World War I in August 1914 postponed its use. Nevertheless, Marie resolved not to abandon the laboratory in the event of a German attack on Paris.

Marie was determined to use her talents to assist in France's war effort. She foresaw the value of X-ray technology in front-line hospitals. Although Marie had never used X rays in her research, she understood the phenomenon and its value in medicine. She made X-ray equipment available and trained its operators. She collected the equipment and donations necessary to make the first mobile X-ray vehicle. She equipped twenty such vehicles, nicknamed "little Curies," and personally used one of them at the forward hospitals. She also was instrumental in installing 200 X-ray rooms in French hospitals. Seventeen-year-old Irène had been trained as a nurse and as an X-ray technician and became a trainer of other technicians.

Marie was happy that after the war, Poland was again a free country. But the war had had detrimental effects on her life: She was drained physically; the overexposure to X rays had affected her health; she had spent most of her money in donations to the French war effort; and her scientific work had been interrupted.

Nevertheless, Marie continued to do research. Her work was hampered, though, by the cataracts that had developed in both eyes and by a nearly continuous humming in her ears. She tried to keep working by using thick glasses; placing bold, colored signs on her instruments; and writing her lecture notes in large letters. Fearing that eventual blindness would end her career, Marie tried to keep her condition a secret. After four eye operations from 1923 to 1930, she was able to return to her work in the laboratory.

In 1922, breaking the tradition that had barred women and research scientists, the French Academy of Medicine elected Marie to their society. They honored her for her part in the discovery of radium and in the advancement of Curietherapy. Then in 1923, the French parliament unanimously voted Marie an annual pension of forty thousand francs. She also received annual payments from a fund in the United States. At last, Marie's money worries were over!

Marie had become the symbol of radium research and Curietherapy. Although she did not enjoy her celebrity status, she took advantage of it to raise funds for the scientific research of radium and its medical uses.

In 1921 Marie visited the United States in return for one gram of radium (then worth more than $150 000) for research at the Institute of Radium in Paris. The American public acclaimed her not only for her achievements but also for the attitude that Eve once characterized as her "scorn for gain, devotion to an intellectual passion, and a desire to serve" (Curie 1938, p. 328). Marie Curie made a strong impression with her thin, frail form; her plain black dress; her gray hair pulled tightly back; and her face "so locked and shuttered" (Curie 1938, p. 348).

Marie and Bronya worked together to plan and raise funds to build an Institute of Radium in Warsaw in their poverty-stricken homeland. They donated a large part of their own personal savings to make their dream a reality. In 1925 Marie returned in triumph to Warsaw to lay the cornerstone of the institute. Marie made a second tour of the United States in 1929 to accept a donation of another gram of radium for the treatment of cancer at the institute in Warsaw. She made her last visit to Poland in 1932 to attend the opening ceremonies of the Radium Institute of Warsaw.

Marie also worked to expand the institute in Paris and encouraged new scientists. Later in life, she focused her energies on directing research and teaching. She took pride in guiding the progress of the scientists on the staff.

In 1926 Irène married Frédéric Joliot, a gifted young scientist at the Institute of Radium. In 1934, under Marie's direction, Irène and Frédéric discovered that by bombarding certain materials with rays, they could produce new radioactive elements not found in nature. These new elements became the source of artificial radioactivity.

Even at sixty-five, Marie Curie continued to work twelve to fourteen hours each day. Eve observed that by then her mother's face was "quite pale, worn and aged by fatigue" (Curie 1938, p. 355). But Marie did not regret the way of life she had chosen. She once said (Curie 1938, p. 357),

> It isn't necessary to lead such an anti-natural existence as mine. I have given a great deal of time to science because I wanted to, because I loved research…. What I want for women and young girls is a simple family life and some work that will interest them.

Marie Curie died at age sixty-six in 1934. Her health had eroded from her long exposure to radium and the fatiguing nature of her work. Until her death, Marie had always considered that there was more for her to do and investigate. She was buried in the Curie family crypt, above the coffin of her beloved Pierre.

After Marie's death, Irène and Frédéric shared the 1935 Nobel Prize in chemistry for their production of new radioactive elements. Both Joliots died in the 1950s as a result of overexposure to radiation.

Guy Weaser
Culver Academies
Culver, Indiana

Suggested Reading

Birch, Beverly. *Marie Curie: The Polish Scientist Who Discovered Radium and Its Life-Saving Properties*. Milwaukee, Wis.: Gareth Stevens, 1988.

Curie, Eve. *Madame Curie: A Biography*. Translated by Vincent Sheean. Garden City, N.Y.: Doubleday, Doran & Co., 1938.

Grady, Sean. *The Importance of Marie Curie*. San Diego: Lucent Books, 1992.

Henry, Joanne Landers. *Marie Curie: Discoverer of Radium*. New York: Macmillan Co., 1966.

Pflaum, Rosalynd. *Grand Obsession: Madame Curie and Her World*. New York: Doubleday Dell Publishing, 1989.

Emmy Noether

—Algebraist for All Times

According to Ann Landers, the most useful bit of advice for all humanity would be "Expect trouble as an inevitable part of life, and when it comes, look it squarely in the eye and say, 'I will be bigger than you. You cannot defeat me.'" Although Ann Landers's comment was made years after Emmy Noether died, this bit of wisdom easily could have been given by this great mathematician. As a woman, Emmy had to receive special permission not only to take a university examination in Germany in 1900 but even to audit classes. Emmy's university lectures had to be announced under a male colleague's name, not under her name, and when she was finally given classes to teach, she received little salary. Since she was Jewish, her teaching privilege was revoked. When the Nazis rose to power, she was forced to leave the country. Because of her gender, her religion, and her liberal political opinions, Emmy Noether was denied a first-class professorship in Germany. Despite all these obstacles, Emmy never complained. The story of Emmy Noether is the story of a warm, unselfish, undaunted woman who loved her work.

Emmy's mother, Ida Amalie Kaufman Noether, was born in 1852 and grew up on an estate in Cologne. Although Ida's father died when she was fourteen, her family was wealthy enough to support Ida and her ten brothers and sisters. Ida excelled in music and enjoyed playing the piano. Emmy's father, Max Noether, was born in 1844 in Mannheim. When he was fourteen, Max came down with infantile paralysis, more commonly known as polio. At the onset of the disease, Max could barely move, and he had a lengthy recovery. Although he regained most of his movement, Max never regained the full use of one of his legs. Because of his illness, he had a private tutor. Max received a liberal education in literature and history and even studied astronomy. In 1868 he attended the University of Heidelberg, where he received a Ph.D. in mathematics. In 1875 he moved to Erlangen and became a full professor at the University of Erlangen in 1888.

The first of four children, Emmy was born to Ida and Max on 23 March 1882. The family eventually included her three brothers—Fritz, Alfred, and Gustav. They lived in a large second-floor apartment in the town of Erlangen. All the Noether children were excellent students.

Emmy had a happy and secure childhood. Her classmates and teachers considered her warm, friendly, easygoing, and clever. She was one of a few students who attended Jewish religion classes. Although she took piano lessons, Emmy did not excel in music as her mother had; she did, however, enjoy dancing. At home, she helped her mother with the housework and the cooking.

Emmy attended the Stadtischen Hoheren Tochterschule in Erlangen for eight years. She liked to study languages. She did not let a slight lisp and nearsightedness keep her from becoming proficient in French and English. After finishing secondary school, Emmy passed tests that would have allowed her to teach French and English at educational institutions for girls, but she decided to continue her education. She wanted to attend the University of Erlangen, where her father taught.

In 1898, the Academic Senate of the University of Erlangen declared that the admission of women to the university would "overthrow all academic order." Many traditional male educators felt that the presence of women at universities would be a distraction to the men. However, in 1900, when Emmy was eighteen, the university made an exception, and she received permission to attend lectures. According to the registry from the University of Erlangen for that year, only 2 of the 986 students were women. Emmy continued to attend lectures until 1902. On 14 July 1903 she passed the matura examinations (qualifying examinations for university admission) at the royal Realgymnasium in Nürnberg. Emmy then entered the University of Göttingen for one semester. She returned to the University of Erlangen in 1904, when it became officially possible for a woman to enroll, attend lectures, and take examinations—finally receiving the same rights as male students. Emmy listed mathematics as her only course of study. With Paul Gordon, a well-known mathematician and friend of the family, as her advisor, Emmy completed her doctoral dissertation in 1907. Her doctorate was conferred the following year.

Being a woman did not prevent Emmy from becoming a mathematician, but it did make it difficult for her to find a job equal to her capabilities. She was as free as any man: unmarried, childless, and requiring little money. But because Emmy was a woman, she was unable to obtain a regular position. From 1908 until 1915, Emmy worked at the Mathematical Institute in Erlangen without pay. Besides carrying out her own research, she would sometimes substitute as a lecturer for her father at the university because it had become extremely difficult for him to get around as he grew older.

In 1908 Emmy was selected a member of the Italian organization Circolo Matematico di Palermo, and she became a member of the Deutschen Mathematiker-Vereinigung, the German Association of Mathematicians, in 1909. Emmy enjoyed going to the meetings, giving presentations, and especially talking about mathematics. Although she was often the only female mathematician present, these sessions gave her an opportunity to exchange ideas and to gain inspiration.

In 1916 Emmy moved to Göttingen, the principal center for mathematics in Germany—perhaps in all of Europe. She was welcomed enthusiastically by David Hilbert and Felix Klein, prominent members of the mathematics faculty. By this time Emmy had published six mathematical research papers and had not yet received any pay for her work. David Hilbert tried to get her a paid position at the University of Göttingen. He even spoke out at faculty meetings in favor of having the university hire her: "I do not see that the sex of the candidate is an argument against her admission as Privadozent [teacher]. After all, we are a university, not a bathing establishment" (Weyl 1935, p. 207). But others would not listen. They said, "Must the soldiers, returning from the deprivations and discipline of war, now find themselves being lectured at the feet of a woman?" (Weyl 1935, p. 207). Although unable to change the rules, Hilbert was able to allow Emmy to lecture. He had to announce her lectures under his name, however, and she was not paid for any of them.

After 1919 the rules were relaxed, and Emmy was given an unofficial associate professorship. She received a small salary and could officially teach algebra, give examinations, and supervise dissertations. However, she received none of the fringe benefits or pension rights given to the male professors. Yet she did not complain; she was happy doing what she loved—mathematics.

In her lectures, Emmy took an abstract approach to mathematics. She would allow the students to discover possible solutions to the problems. Some students enjoyed this approach, whereas others wished to be presented with clear, definite conclusions. Emmy's style of teaching worked most effectively with gifted students, many of whom went on to become well-known mathematicians. The outstanding students she attracted from many European countries became known as the "Noether boys." Emmy was always available to her students, instructing them from her wealth of mathematical knowledge. Whenever she discovered talented students, Emmy would help them get assistantships or give them whatever else they might need to continue their education.

Unconcerned about material goods, Emmy purchased new clothes only when friends suggested that it was time to do so. It was thought that she bought men's shoes because they were sturdier—she was an avid walker. Once when she was walking with a group of students, someone noticed that her umbrella was in poor condition. When a student suggested that she have it repaired, Emmy replied that that would be impossible because on clear days she would forget it and on rainy days she would need it. Emmy usually ate at the same restaurant, at the same time, in the same place—often having the same meal. Mathematics was first and foremost in her life, and her sole pursuit.

Emmy spent winter 1928–29 as a visiting professor in Moscow, where she taught a course on abstract algebra and led a seminar on algebraic geometry. She enjoyed her time there, feeling very much at home. During her stay, Emmy became interested in the country and its people, particularly the Soviet students.

After the esteemed mathematician Hermann Weyl received an appointment at the University of Göttingen in 1930, he tried to get a better position for Emmy. He was embarrassed to have a position above hers, knowing that Emmy was his superior in mathematics. But his attempt failed. Tradition and prejudice were too strong to permit a change, even in the interest of scientific merit or greatness.

The year 1932 was Emmy's last full year in Germany. During this time she received the Alfred Ackerman Teubner Memorial Prize for the advancement of the mathematical sciences. The prize for her scientific achievement was 500 reichmarks—approximately $120.

Emmy was gratified when her colleagues at Göttingen held a celebration for her fiftieth birthday. Although a modest and humble person, Emmy enjoyed being recognized by her fellow algebraists. She was particularly delighted when one of her colleagues, Helmut Hasse, dedicated a paper to her.

Also in 1932, Emmy was asked to lecture at a general session of the International Mathematical Congress in Zurich. This honor was a high point in her career. Of twenty-one lecturers, Emmy was the only woman. A summary of Emmy's work was read at this meeting.

By this time the popularity and power of the Nazi party had increased. On 30 January 1933, Hitler became chancellor of Germany. At the University of Göttingen pro-Nazi activity had accelerated, and swastikas and brown shirts were a common sight in the classroom.

Hitler announced the beginning of the Third Reich on 31 March 1933. Shortly after that he passed the Enabling Act, allowing him to make decrees autonomously. As a result, the lives of the Jewish people changed dramatically; they were systematically dismissed from German life.

On 7 April 1933, Emmy received a notice from a representative of the Prussian Minister for Sciences, Arts, and Public Education that her right to teach had been withdrawn. Many other professors received the same notification. Still, Emmy's involvement in her beloved mathematics continued. She would hold informal meetings to discuss mathematics. It did not bother her when a student dressed in a secret police uniform attended one of these sessions in her apartment. Hermann Weyl wrote of Emmy, "Her courage, her frankness, her unconcern about her own fate, her conciliatory spirit was in the midst of all the hatred and meanness, despair and sorrow surrounding us, a moral solace."

In 1933 many fine German-Jewish mathematicians and scientists, including Emmy Noether, were forced to leave Germany. Many of them sought refuge in the United States. Committees were formed to help them find new positions commensurate with their abilities. Emmy was invited to be a visiting professor at Bryn Mawr College in Pennsylvania for the academic year 1933–34. In time she received a regular faculty appointment.

Fortunately, Emmy was a self-sufficient individual who had the ability to adapt to new situations. She was warmly received by the Bryn Mawr community. Her English was satisfactory, and everyone enjoyed her. Although Emmy knew very little about the college, the Bryn Mawr community knew a good deal about her and considered themselves fortunate to have her working among them.

In summer 1934 Emmy returned to Germany. Few of the people she knew were still there. Emmy found the situation very different from the one she had left. Some of her former colleagues even avoided her; she decided, therefore, to leave her native country and move her belongings to the United States.

Emmy again taught at Bryn Mawr during the 1934–35 academic year. On 10 April 1935, she underwent surgery for the removal of a tumor. The doctors considered her a risk because she had high blood pressure. Emmy did well the first three days following surgery, but on the fourth day her temperature rose to 109 degrees. She lapsed into unconsciousness and died on 14 April. Her physicians were not sure what had happened; she may have had an unusual viral infection. Emmy was cremated, and her ashes were buried at Bryn Mawr.

Although Emmy Noether was not recognized in Germany as a great mathematician while she lived, the scientific world recognized the importance of her work after her death. Indeed, a large area of algebra was profoundly changed by her methods. In 1958, on the fiftieth anniversary of Emmy's receipt of her doctoral degree, the University of Erlangen had a reunion of many of her students to discuss her impact on mathematics. In 1960 the city of Erlangen named a street, Noetherstrasse, after her. At the 1964 World's Fair, one room was devoted to mathematics, giving a brief survey of the history of mathematics. Of the eighty pictures of mathematicians displayed, only one was of a woman, Emmy Noether. And on 27 February 1982, a Noether memorial tablet was unveiled in the Mathematical Institute at the University of Erlangen. In the United States later in that year, Emmy's 100th birthday was celebrated by the American Mathematical Society with a conference at Bryn Mawr.

Emmy Noether is remembered as a great mathematician, a great scholar, and an extraordinary teacher. She loved mathematics and people. They were her life.

Susan E. Clark
Saint Matthew Cathedral School
South Bend, Indiana

Suggested Reading

Brewer, James W., and Martha K. Smith. *Emmy Noether: A Tribute to Her Life and Work.* New York: Marcel Dekker, 1981.

Dick, Auguste. *Emmy Noether 1882–1935.* Boston: Birkhäuser Boston, 1981.

Sally, Judith, and Bhama Srinivasan. *Emmy Noether in Bryn Mawr.* New York: Springer-Verlag New York, 1983.

Reference

Weyl, Hermann. "Emmy Noether." *Scripta Mathematica* 8 (July 1935).

Barbara McClintock

—Unlocking the Mysteries of Chromosomes

Barbara said, "I do not want to go to school today because I do not like my teacher." Her mother replied, "You may stay at home as long as you feel that way." Would your parents react this way? Probably not, but this conversation demonstrates the nonconformist attitudes of the McClintock family in the early 1900s.

As a child, Barbara McClintock had the remarkable talent of completely absorbing herself in whatever she was studying. She also tended to pursue activities as she pleased, regardless of what anyone else thought of her. This way of living—pursuing wholeheartedly precisely what she wanted and being true to herself—was the way Barbara McClintock conducted her life, with uncommon results. Her brilliance—some people considered her a genius—was secondary to her personality traits. Without both her intelligence and her strong character, it is questionable that Barbara could have achieved the scientific advances that made her one of the most important female scientists of the twentieth century.

Barbara McClintock was born on 16 June 1902 in Hartford, Connecticut. She grew up in Brooklyn, New York, at a time when women were finally being admitted to undergraduate and also some graduate schools in this country. But the glass ceiling, the invisible barrier beyond which women could not expect to rise in their professions, remained low. Women with a college education, even a doctorate, were expected either to get married or to teach at a women's college. In scientific research, a woman usually worked in her husband's laboratory or as a laboratory assistant. Women were not appointed to professorates at most colleges and universities. Professional societies were for the most part not open to them. At this time most female scientists either married and raised a family, taught other women, or worked as assistants to male scientists. Few other jobs were readily available to women in science.

Barbara's childhood years were certainly unconventional. Her parents, New England born and bred, were strong-willed individuals. In 1898, Sara Handy, Barbara's mother, married Thomas Henry McClintock, a medical student. Sara's father, a Congregational minister, disapproved of the marriage, so the young married couple were on their own. They often faced financial difficulties while Dr. McClintock was establishing his practice. Mrs. McClintock, a musician, contributed to the family's finances by giving piano lessons in her home.

The McClintocks had unusual ideas about child rearing. They raised each child to pursue her or his individual talents and were not afraid to allow the children to be different. Dr. McClintock in particular did not have much tolerance for the schooling practices of the day. Believing that six hours of schoolwork was enough, he told the teachers not to assign his children homework. He wanted them to have time to pursue other interests and allowed them to stay at home, sometimes for an entire semester, rather than attend school. Following rules did not seem to be a top priority in the McClintock household. And following the rules was never high on Barbara McClintock's list, either. This tendency to ignore the rules and do as she pleased sometimes resulted in problems for Barbara in her adult years.

Barbara was a curious child who was interested in how things worked. Once, after requesting some tools, Barbara became upset because she was given child-sized tools rather than the real thing. A tomboy, she had her mother make her short trousers, or knickers, so she could play games and climb trees with the boys. Barbara studied music, but her mother discontinued her lessons because Barbara became too intense. This ability to concentrate on a single subject would later contribute greatly to Barbara McClintock's success as a scientist.

Despite missing so much school, Barbara was an excellent student at both the grade school and the high school she attended in New York City. After graduating from high school at age sixteen, Barbara wanted to go to college. Her mother prevented her from doing so because Mrs. McClintock was opposed to higher education for women.

During World War I, Barbara's father served in Europe as an army doctor. Family finances were again strained, so Barbara worked in an employment agency. As soon as her job was over for the day, she headed for the library, determined to educate herself.

As with many of the few women who had excelled in mathematics and science before her, Barbara received encouragement from her father to continue her education. When Dr. McClintock returned in summer 1918, he persuaded his wife to let Barbara go to college. She chose to attend Cornell University in Ithaca, New York, because the agricultural college did not charge tuition.

During her first few years at Cornell, socializing and exploring various fields of learning became Barbara's passions. Three reasons in particular accounted for her excitement: First of all, Cornell was a beautiful campus located on a steep hill overlooking one of the Finger Lakes, Lake Cayuga. Second, Barbara was free to pursue any field of study that she wished. She took many courses and completed them if she liked them or dropped them if she did not. Third, Barbara was exposed to a diverse student body that included people of various religions and nationalities. For the first time in her life, she had an active social life. She played tennis and entertained other students on her banjo. She was even elected president of the freshman class.

All was not perfect, however. When Barbara was invited to join a sorority, she declined because she was appalled by its exclusivity. In particular, the sororities did not ask her Jewish friends to join. Barbara's aversion to clubs and societies continued throughout her life. She joined such groups only when absolutely necessary for her professional growth, and then she did not attend their meetings.

The turning point in Barbara's life came in her junior year, when she took a course in genetics. She was so fascinated by the subject that she decided that genetics would be her area of study. In the 1920s genetics was a new science. It was the most exciting field in biology.

At Cornell genetics was taught in the Department of Plant Breeding. The head of the department was the famous corn geneticist Rollins A. Emerson. Rollins attracted the best male students in the field of plant breeding. He attracted Barbara McClintock, too, but she had to enter the department through the back door. At the time Barbara was applying to graduate schools, the Department of Plant Breeding did not accept female students. Barbara's work in cytology (the study of cells) in the Department of Botany had also been highly successful. The botany department accepted female graduate students, so Barbara enrolled there. She majored in cytology, with a minor in genetics. This blending of two fields would serve her well. Her experience is an example of how a situation that seems to impede advancement can turn out to be fortuitous.

In graduate school from 1923 to 1927, Barbara increased her considerable skills as a cytologist. She focused on studying the chromosomes inside the nucleus—the control center of a cell. Her ability to prepare slides of chromosomes soon surpassed that of her professors. At that time, the results of studies of fruit-fly chromosomes led geneticists to suspect that genes are located on the chromosomes of a cell. Genes are hereditary factors that are passed from parents to offspring and determine the organism's appearance and makeup. Barbara decided to study the corn plant, known to scientists as *Zea mays*, or *maize*. Thus began her lifelong research on the chromosomes of maize.

Scientists knew that maize has ten chromosomes, but they could not tell them apart. Barbara determined the specific size of each chromosome from smallest to largest, so they could be differentiated at all stages of plant-cell reproduction. She noticed that the shapes of chromosomes differed according to the characteristics of the corn plant they came from. This observation suggested that when the shapes of the chromosomes were slightly different, different forms of genes were present, causing variations in the plants.

By the age of twenty-five, Barbara had published her findings in scientific journals. Her work was at the forefront of the new field of cytogenetics—the blending of cytology with genetics. Barbara became absorbed in deciphering the genetics of maize and in determining how the characteristics of maize are inherited. Her ability to focus and to block out everything else allowed her to make observations and ask questions no one else did. It helped her excel in her field. Early in her career, she was highly respected. Later she made discoveries that were so advanced that they were not properly recognized until thirty years later.

After Barbara received her Ph.D., she became an instructor at Cornell and continued to study maize. She was interested in how genes that are on the same chromosome—linked genes—are inherited. Her research required that she grow plants in the summer and study the chromosomes in the seed (the offspring) in the fall and winter. The work with corn, which reproduces only once a year, was slow compared with work with fruit flies. Fruit flies—the other organism popular with geneticists at the time—reproduce many generations in a year. Barbara also had to learn to breed plants to grow her own corn. This facet of her work put her in the company of the young corn researchers who had been attracted to Cornell's Department of Plant Breeding.

This group of exceptional corn geneticists included Marcus Rhodes, Charles Burnham, and George Beadle, all under the direction of Rollins Emerson. Marcus Rhodes's interest in corn cytogenetics developed largely from his conversations with Barbara when he first came to Cornell. He later had an illustrious career in research and teaching. He understood the goals of Barbara's research and became her friend for life. George Beadle later turned to molecular genetics. In 1958, he, Edward Tatum, and

Joshua Lederberg shared the Nobel Prize in physiology and medicine for their one-gene–one-enzyme hypothesis. Beadle, too, recognized Barbara's brilliance in cytology and later requested her help in this area. Emerson was already a famous scientist. Barbara was to become as famous as her male colleagues—it just took a little longer.

It must have been strange at first for these men to have a brilliant, skilled, intense woman growing corn with them and discussing their research. Just as Barbara had been accepted earlier as a tomboy by the boys in her neighborhood, she was accepted later as a colleague by this remarkable group of men. Emerson and Rhodes helped her advance in her career, as did other men who respected her intelligence. Until 1947, Cornell's only female assistant professor—the lowest professorial rank—taught in the home economics department. (Women did not even have the right to vote until 1920.) Barbara McClintock knew that female scientists faced obstacles in their careers. Through her contacts with male scientists, she attained positions that enabled her to work on her cytogenetic corn research.

While an instructor at Cornell, Barbara influenced the career of Harriet Creighton, another young woman who had just arrived at Cornell for graduate work. In a short time the two of them produced the definitive paper on genes and chromosomes that made them both famous. Barbara was interested in studying crossing-over, a phenomenon long suspected by other geneticists but never substantiated by research. Crossing-over occurs when chromosomes duplicate during cell division. Prior to separating, the arms of the chromosomes become entangled with one another and sometimes break and change places. In this way linked genes can become separated from one another. Crossing-over is one way in which genetic characteristics get mixed up between generations.

Barbara and Harriet performed an experiment in one generation of corn that supported the hypothesis of crossing-over. Their findings were published in the *Proceedings of the National Academy of Sciences*. This paper reported their proof that chromosomes are made up of genes. Its publication established both women as well-respected research scientists.

After this success, Barbara's first try at a permanent job did not work out. Barbara's personality did not suit her for the position, and she experienced discrimination because she was a woman. Through the efforts of Lewis Stadler, an important scientist, she was offered an appointment as an assistant professor at the University of Missouri. Barbara's research on the ways in which broken chromosomes heal themselves went well during her five years at Missouri. But she soon realized that her position as a faculty member was not working out. She was kept from attending faculty meetings, from hearing about new job opportunities, and from being promoted. It seemed as if the administration wanted her only for the recognition her research brought to the university.

Barbara's unconventional behavior also posed problems. The administration had not expected that their female assistant professor would climb in windows when she had forgotten her keys or that she would encourage graduate students to work past the eleven o'clock curfew. And they did not appreciate her failure to start classes for the term at the appointed time when it did not fit her schedule. As usual, Barbara followed her own schedule, not one imposed on her. Her penchant for disregarding the rules had surfaced once again. Barbara took a leave of absence from the University of Missouri in 1941 and never returned.

Despite her employment problems, Barbara was by this time recognized as a famous scientist. Her peers cited her research in the cytogenetics of maize and considered her microscopy techniques second to none. In 1939 she was elected vice-president of the Genetics Society of America and later became the first female president of the society. In 1944 she was elected to the National Academy of Sciences—the third woman to be so honored. Clearly, she was known as a leading geneticist, but in 1941 she did not have a laboratory and had not yet begun the work that was to earn her the greatest distinction.

Through discussions with Marcus Rhodes, Barbara learned about the Cold Spring Harbor Research Center on Long Island in New York State. She received a summer appointment there in 1941 and never left except for short assignments. It was a perfect place for her to work. Barbara lived a simple life there, separated from the consumerism that overran the United States after World War II. She needed little besides her laboratory, a two-room apartment, and a place to grow her corn. The study of maize became her whole life, and she loved it. She was doing exactly what she wanted to do. Barbara studied mutations in maize chromosomes that behaved strangely. Her discoveries would not be appropriately recognized for thirty years.

Barbara slowly began to realize that some genes control how a plant looks and that these genes are controlled by other genes. She soon discovered that the controlling genes move from chromosome to chromosome in a process called *transposition* and that they are themselves controlled. Her research was complex and was not understood by most other cytogeneticists. Her conclusions were inconsistent with the accepted gene model of the time. According to that model, genes were fixed on the chromosome and did not move. McClintock's "jumping genes" were considered heresy. In 1951 she presented her work to other scientists at a symposium at Cold Spring Harbor, but her research was not understood, accepted, or cited by other scientists. Next she presented her work at smaller conferences and published it in the journal *Genetics* in 1953. In every instance the response was the same: rejection or indifference.

Barbara continued her research for many years, gathering evidence for genetic control of genes by genes that move around the chromosomes. Barbara published her findings in the annual reports of the Carnegie Institution of Washington, whose Department of Genetics was located at Cold Spring Harbor. She refused to be discouraged by the lack of acceptance from her peers. Barbara used to say that she could not wait to get up in the morning and begin working in the laboratory. She would work all day and well into the night—then she would begin again. During this time, Barbara remained absolutely certain that her research was sound. She did all the laborious data analysis herself and was sure that her conclusions were correct. Eventually, the rest of the world accepted her findings, but not before some remarkable discoveries were made in molecular biology.

In 1953 James Watson and Francis Crick described the double-helix structure of the deoxyribonucleic acid, or DNA, molecule. Genes consist of DNA. In 1960 Jacques-Lucien Monod and François Jacob published their findings about a system of gene regulation in the bacterium *Escherichia coli* that was similar to one reported by Barbara in 1951. She wrote a paper about the similarities and published it in the *American Naturalist*. In 1965 Monod and Jacob received a Nobel Prize for their work. Although they gave credit to Barbara McClintock for having found a gene-regulation system similar to theirs ten years earlier, the rest of the scientific community still ignored her work.

Gradually scientists accumulated other evidence of the instability of chromosomes. They had to acknowledge that Barbara McClintock had been right all along. Slowly the scientific community recognized her contributions. She was appointed professor at large at her alma mater in 1965. Next she received the 1970 National Medal of Science. Barbara continued to do research and began again to publish her findings. In 1981, thirty years after her first attempt to explain transposition, Barbara McClintock received eight awards, including the Albert Lasker Basic Medical Research Award and a $60 000-a-year lifetime award from the MacArthur Foundation. Barbara was unimpressed with these belated honors and shied away from publicity. But an even higher honor awaited her.

In 1983 Barbara McClintock became the seventh woman to win a Nobel Prize since the award was instituted in 1901. She was the first woman to win it independently in the category of physiology and medicine. Barbara did not want the attention and was happy when the presentation was over so she could return to her research. On the videotape *Barbara McClintock—Pioneer of Modern Genetics* (McCormack 1990), Barbara appears as a confident but humble elderly woman who seems a bit uncomfortable with all the attention she is getting. She would prefer, she says, not to have had so much time spent in honoring her.

Despite many obstacles, Barbara had pursued exactly what she wanted and eventually received the highest honor in her field. Did celebrity and wealth change her life? Barbara moved into a larger apartment and bought a Honda automobile so as to get around more easily. Since Barbara was never one to accumulate things, her life changed very little otherwise. She returned to Cold Spring Harbor and her maize research.

Characteristically, Barbara was not bitter about the job discrimination she had faced or the years of waiting for acceptance of her discoveries. She was grateful for the opportunities she had been afforded, especially to do research at Cold Spring Harbor. She always had a warm place in her heart for Cornell, too. Barbara returned there many times to give lectures. Barbara McClintock is not considered a champion of women's rights, but she understood the significance of her achievement, particularly for other women. For that reason she endured the unwanted publicity and relinquished the time it took from her work.

Many lessons can be learned from Barbara McClintock's life and work. Her example teaches people to be true to themselves. Despite what others thought she should do, Barbara did what she wanted to do and what she felt was right. For example, although she dated and formed close relationships with men at Cornell, she never felt that marriage was right for her, and she never second-guessed her decision to remain single. She valued convenience more than pleasing others. She was the first woman at Cornell to wear short hair because caring for long hair required too much time.

Barbara was well served by her characteristic confidence in her abilities to ask questions; to concentrate on a problem; to work long, hard hours for extended periods; to organize and analyze data; and most important, to trust her intuition. Barbara would not have minded being called a "workaholic." Her research was her enjoyment, her life, and what she most wanted to do.

Barbara McClintock died on 2 September 1992 in Huntington, New York. At ninety years, she had lived almost ten years after having received her Nobel Prize. She conducted research on maize until the time of her death.

Barbara's discoveries about maize chromosomes have important implications for future research. Her major work describes maize genes that move from chromosome to chromosome, genes that control other genes, and genes that are influenced by environmental factors outside the cell.

These same mechanisms of gene behavior are found in other organisms, including humans. No longer do scientists believe that genetic information always stays put on the chromosome and that genetic information flows only from the gene to the cell.

Research is now focusing on how an organism develops from a single fertilized cell into an adult. Scientists are interested in the role of controlling genes in determining when other genes start influencing the organism's development. Scientific investigation in the following areas is progressing in directions suggested by Barbara and others: cancer research, research in the resistance of bacteria to antibiotics, and research to improve strains of cereal crops that can feed the growing world population. Clearly, Barbara McClintock's contributions to genetics have had a profound effect on the world community and have made her one of the most important scientists of the twentieth century.

Janice M. Ivkovich
The Stanley Clark School
South Bend, Indiana

Suggested Reading

"Barbara McClintock: The World Has Finally Caught Up to Her Ideas." *Science Digest*, February 1984, p. 29.

Clark, Matt, and Kristine Mortensen. "Genetic Pioneer Wins a Nobel." *Newsweek*, 24 October 1983, p. 97.

Keller, Evelyn Fox. *A Feeling for the Organism*. New York: W. H. Freeman & Co., 1983.

Kittredge, Mary. *Barbara McClintock*. New York: Chelsea House Publishers, 1991.

McClintock, Barbara. "The Significance of Responses of the Genome to Challenge." *Science*, 16 November 1984, pp. 792–801.

McCormack, Todd, producer. *Barbara McClintock—Pioneer of Modern Genetics*. Videotape from Nobel Prize series. 1990.

Grace Murray Hopper

—Computer Pioneer and Admiral

A visitor to Grace Hopper's office might have noticed her clock. Was it typical? No, but then neither was Grace Hopper. Grace's clock ran backward—counterclockwise. Its numbers were reversed, too, giving the impression of looking at a clock in the reflection of a mirror. What does this anecdote say about Grace Hopper? She was always looking for a new way of doing something. She refused to accept the statement "But we've always done it that way." Grace also was not one to take no for an answer. Because of her creativity and persistence, she is known as Amazing Grace, Grandmother of the Computer Age.

On 9 December 1906 Grace Brewster Murray was born in New York City to Mary Campbell Van Horne Murray and Walter Fletcher Murray.

Grace, named after her mother's lifelong friend, Grace Brewster, was the oldest of three children. Her sister, Mary, was born three years later, followed by her brother, Roger, two years after that.

Grace's favorite pastime was reading. She always put books on her Christmas wish list. One series of books that her mother enjoyed was passed down to Grace. Grace, too, liked these books that featured a little girl who participated in the founding of each of the great cities of the United States. Her other favorites included the *Just So Stories*, by Rudyard Kipling, and *The Secret Garden*, by Frances Burnett.

Grace enjoyed playing with toys. Among her favorites were several building sets and a dollhouse. Her Structiron Construction Set was composed of nuts, bolts, metal pieces, and an electrical motor, so she could build elevators and electric vehicles. She also liked a stone set imported from Germany, which included plans similar to blueprints. When Grace carefully followed the plans, she could make churches and other buildings. She was also interested in playing with peg-lock blocks that had openings in their edges, allowing them to lock together. Grace especially liked the locking feature because she could make structures that were difficult to knock down. As for her dollhouse, Grace was more interested in making accessories for it than in actually playing with it. She made curtains, furniture, and other decorative items for her dollhouse.

The Murray family often spent the summer at her grandfather's cottage on Lake Wentworth, near Wolfeboro, New Hampshire. The cottage was large, with seven bedrooms to accommodate all the summer guests. Grace would play hide and seek, kick the can, and cops and robbers with her cousins. Every one of the seven bedrooms had an alarm clock in it, and each clock had a round face, two legs, and a bell on top. One day, overcome with curiosity about how the clock worked, Grace took apart one of the clocks but was unable to put it back together. Hoping to learn how to reassemble the first, she took apart another clock, and then another. By the time she was through, Grace had dismantled all seven clocks. After that incident Grace's mother allowed her to disassemble only one clock.

During Grace's childhood, her father suffered from hardening of the arteries in his legs. In the early 1900s medicine was not very advanced. Nothing could be done for so severe a case as her father's except amputation. Both his legs had been amputated by the time Grace was in her first year of high school. Her determined father was able to get around through the use of wooden legs and canes. He even returned to work. His perseverance became a source of inspiration to other amputees as well as to his children. The Murray children worked hard to get A's in school to honor their father.

Mr. Murray believed in equal education for boys and girls. He had observed that many of his friends' daughters had been unable to get jobs because of their lack of training. He encouraged all three of his children to go to college and urged his daughters to work for at least one year after graduation. Because of his illness and the uncertainty about how long he would be able to support his family, Mr. Murray wanted his daughters to be self-sufficient. Even with all his medical problems, he lived to be seventy-five years old. No doubt his strong will and determination had much to do with his long life. Grace learned about the importance of perseverance from her father.

Grace attended private girls' schools, as was common at the time. These schools prepared girls to become ladies. Grace received a double promotion, so she finished Schoonmakers School when she was sixteen. She might have entered college early, but she had failed a Latin examination, and her family decided that she was too young to begin her college career. As a result, in fall 1923 she attended Hartridge School, a college preparatory school in Plainfield, New Jersey. Here Grace was required to take English, Latin, another foreign language, and history or science, as well as singing, calisthenics, gymnastics, and dancing. She also participated in basketball and hockey, performed in two plays, and sang in the glee club.

The founder of Hartridge took an interest in Grace and encouraged her to apply to Vassar. Grace never seriously considered another college; she entered Vassar in fall 1924.

Grace was determined to make the most of her college education. When she attended Vassar, the students could audit as many classes as they wanted. Grace audited all the beginning classes in the sciences as well as in business and economics. Since she could explain ideas well, she was asked to tutor other students. She would often use examples the students could easily understand. For instance, to illustrate the concept of displacement, Grace filled a tub with water, marked the water level, and then asked the student to get in and observe the change in level. When the student saw the rise in the water level, she was able to understand the theory of displacement.

In her senior year, Grace was elected to Phi Beta Kappa, the oldest honor society in the United States. In 1928 she graduated with a Bachelor of Arts degree in mathematics and physics and won a Vassar fellowship that allowed her to go on to graduate school. Without it she probably would not have continued her education, since her parents still had two children to put through college. Grace attended Yale and received a Master of Arts degree in mathematics in 1930. In that same year she was asked to join Sigma Xi, an honor society that recognizes the outstanding research achievements of scientists.

Grace Murray married Vincent Foster Hopper on 15 June 1930. She had met him in summer 1923 at Wolfeboro. Vincent had graduated from Princeton in 1927 with highest honors. In 1928 he received a master's degree from Princeton and went on to teach English at New York University's School of Commerce. He and Grace settled in New York City. Grace accepted a mathematics teaching position at Vassar for $800 a year. She taught algebra, trigonometry, and calculus. Later she developed courses in statistics, probability, and analysis. In 1934 she received a Ph.D. in mathematics from Yale. Attaining this degree was considered quite an accomplishment for anyone—but especially for a woman. Only seven doctorates in mathematics were granted by Yale in the three years following Grace's graduation.

When the United States entered World War II, many Americans came forward to support their country. Grace and her family were among them. Grace's husband and brother joined the United States Army Air Corps as volunteers. Her father worked on the Selective Service Board, her mother on the Ration Board, and her sister in the General Electric plant making proximity fuses, fuses that set off a bomb as it gets close to its target.

Grace, too, wished to contribute to the cause: she wanted to join the United States Navy. But there was a problem. She was too old to enlist, and the government officials thought she could better serve the war effort by teaching mathematics. The only way Grace could enter the service was to get special permission to do so or to quit her job and stay unemployed for six months. She managed to get special permission. There was still another problem—her weight. According to navy regulations, a woman five feet six inches tall needed to weigh at least one hundred twenty-one pounds to join the navy. Grace weighed only one hundred five pounds. But again she obtained special permission. In December 1943 she was sworn into the United States Naval Reserve. She was then sent to the United States Naval Reserve Midshipman's School for Women. To stay in the navy, Grace had to graduate from the program. Although she was in class with students of the same age as those she had been teaching, Grace graduated first in her class and was commissioned a lieutenant on 27 June 1944.

Grace was assigned by the navy to work on the Bureau of Ordnance Computation Project at Harvard University. On 2 July 1944 she reported to Harvard to work with the Mark I computer. The Mark I was conceived by Howard Aiken, a commander in the United States Naval Reserve who had gone to Harvard to earn his Ph.D. The research project he was working on required time-consuming, complex calculations. He looked for a machine to do the work. Aiken had the idea, and International Business Machines (IBM) had the technology. He convinced Harvard and IBM to build the first large-scale digital computer—the Mark I. But by the time the computer was completed, the United States was involved in World War II. It was crucial to complete the complex calculations necessary to aim the navy guns accurately. Grace helped program the Mark I to get these calculations for the navy. She worked with three other officers and four enlisted men to keep the machine programmed and running twenty-four hours a day to provide the Pentagon with the needed information.

The Mark I was eight feet high and eight feet deep, with a fifty-one-foot rotary shaft running its length. The shaft was driven by a four-horsepower motor located between two panels at the back of the computer. It weighed five tons and had approximately eight hundred thousand parts and over five hundred miles of wire. It was enclosed in glass and was electromechanical. Although run by electricity, it contained a large number of bulky, mechanical switches that opened and closed during operation, making a continual clicking noise. Instructions were given to the computer by punched IBM cards. The Mark I could perform three additions each second and handle numbers up to twenty-three digits in length. It was hailed as a modern mechanical miracle. Grace Hopper thought it was the "prettiest gadget" she had ever seen and was pleased that a machine finally had been invented to assist the power of the brain rather than the strength of the body. The Mark I became Grace's favorite computer, and later, when it was no longer used, Grace would go to see it at the Smithsonian Institution.

During summer 1945, the Mark II was being built. Because of the war, components were in short supply. Any suitable component that was found was used in the computer. One day when Grace was working on the Mark II, it suddenly stopped running. The crew discovered that a relay had failed. On dismantling it they found a moth that had been beaten to death by the relay. The crew removed the moth with a pair of tweezers and taped it into the logbook. They told Aiken that they had "debugged the computer." This incident is believed to be the origin of the term *debugging*. That moth can still be found in the logbook kept at the Naval Museum at the Naval Surface Weapons Center in Dahlgren, Virginia.

The Mark II computer was five times as fast as the Mark I. It was the first computer that could run two programs at the same time. Grace and her coworkers collected programs that worked and recorded them in a notebook. Since many of these programs concerned mathematics and science problems, only a person knowledgeable in these areas could program the computer. Grace hoped that computers could someday be used by people other than mathematicians and scientists.

In 1945 Grace and Vincent were divorced. In 1946 Grace was forced to leave active duty in the navy because of her age. (She remained in the reserve unit, however.) She then received an offer to return to Vassar to teach mathematics, but instead, she decided to stay at Harvard because, as she observed, "computers were more fun."

In 1949 Grace Hopper began working for Eckert Mauchly Computer Corporation in Philadelphia as a senior mathematician. This company designed and manufactured the first mass-produced commercial computer in 1951. It had many memory devices and used high-speed magnetic tape instead of punched cards. It was only fourteen and one-half feet long, nine feet wide, and seven and one-half feet high. It processed three thousand additions and subtractions each second.

Because of Grace's experience with the computer, she was convinced that a person could program the computer to execute a set of complex instructions. However, few people other than mathematicians and scientists were able to do so because of the technical and painstaking nature of writing *code*, or the basic binary instructions that the computer was capable of carrying out. To make computers easier for more people to use, Grace envisioned developing a computer programming language that could be used and understood by more people. She was certain that a way could be found to translate the programming language into the machine code that could then be "understood" by the computer.

In 1952, Grace completed her first *compiler*, a set of instructions that translates a more natural, humanlike language into a machine code that enables the computer to perform specific functions. The compiler allowed the computer to determine the appropriate instructions needed to perform a series of operations. Previously, a set of instructions specific to each operation had had to be fed into the computer in machine language, or *code*, as needed. This method had led to frequent mistakes.

Although the first computers were able to do only mathematical computations, Grace believed that programming languages and compilers could be developed to perform more complex operations, such as standard business tasks. Grace designed several more compilers, and eventually her persistence resulted in a recognition of the value of compilers and in their widespread use.

Grace's next project was to write computer programs in English. She thought of the letters of the alphabet as other symbols that, like mathematical symbols, could be translated into machine code. Grace and her staff had difficulty convincing others that such translation was possible. Grace believed that a good idea often takes from two to five years to catch on. She thought that people who believe in their ideas should go ahead and try them and worry later about getting permission. It was much easier to apologize later, she observed, than to get permission beforehand—so that is how Grace proceeded.

By 1957 three different programming languages were being used in American computers. Grace believed that only one universal computer language was needed that could be used on any computer and could be understood by people other than mathematicians and computer scientists. Grace kept persevering until her vision became a reality.

On 6 December 1960, UNIVAC and the Radio Corporation of America (RCA) introduced COBOL, which stands for Common Business Oriented Language. The companies demonstrated that COBOL could be used on two different computers. Grace Hopper, of course, participated in this demonstration. In 1962 IBM finally joined UNIVAC and RCA in accepting COBOL as the common programming language. It then became one of the most widely used computer languages in the world, and the United States Department of Defense urged American businesses to accept it. Many had to do so in order to keep doing business with the government. Since COBOL uses English-like sentences, it is easier to understand than other computer languages.

After twenty-three years in the Naval Reserve, Grace was asked to apply for retirement. She did, and on 31 December 1966, she was placed on the Naval Reserve retired list with the rank of commander. Grace later said, "It was the saddest day of my life." Her retirement, however, was brief. The United States Navy asked Grace to return to temporary active duty on 1 August 1967. Her mission was to standardize COBOL for the navy. Under her guidance a navy training manual, *Fundamentals of COBOL*, was published.

Grace has received many awards for her computer expertise. In 1969 she was the first person to receive the Computer Science Man of the Year Award from the Data Processing Management Association. This award recognizes an individual who has made an outstanding contribution to computer science.

In 1971 Sperry Corporation established the Grace Murray Hopper Award. This award is presented annually to a young computer professional who has made a significant contribution to computer science.

In 1973 Grace was given the Legion of Merit, an award originating in the days of George Washington. It is given to military personnel for the performance of outstanding service. Also in 1973 Grace was the first American and the first woman to be made a Distinguished Fellow of the British Computer Society.

Three years later Grace was given the W. Wallace McDowell Award from the Institute of Electrical and Electronic Engineers Computer Society; in 1980 she received the Navy Meritorious Service Medal; and in 1983 she received the American Association of University Women Achievement Award. These acknowledgments are just some of the honors conferred on Grace for her achievements in computer science. She has also received numerous honorary degrees.

Grace Hopper was formally promoted on 15 December 1983 to the rank of commodore by Secretary of the Navy John Lehman at the White House. On 15 November 1984 she was inducted into the Engineering and Science Hall of Fame. Also inducted that day were George Washington Carver and Henry Heimlich. Among the six previous inductees were Jonas Salk and Thomas Edison. Grace is obviously recognized among a highly respected group of innovators.

On 28 July 1987 the Grace Murray Hopper Service Center of the Navy Regional Data Automation Center in San Diego was dedicated. It was named for her "in recognition of her extraordinary contributions to the Navy." Many of Grace's honorary degrees and military citations are displayed in a special room in the center.

Grace was interviewed on *Sixty Minutes* and the *David Letterman Show*. She also served as grand marshal of the 1987 Orange Bowl Parade. But despite all these forms of recognition, Grace Hopper believed that the highest achievement she ever attained was "the privilege and responsibility of serving with true allegiance, very proudly, in the United States Navy." On 8 November 1985 she was promoted to rear admiral. On 14 August 1986 Rear Admiral Hopper retired from the United States Navy. She was awarded the Distinguished Service Medal, the Defense Department's highest honor, given for exceptionally meritorious service to the United States.

Although she retired from the navy at age seventy-nine, Grace then went to work at Digital Equipment Corporation as senior consultant. She was unable to give up what she loved most—"teaching and getting people interested in computers."

In 1991 Grace was awarded the National Medal of Technology by President George Bush. She was the first individual woman to receive it.

On 1 January 1992 Grace Hopper died in Arlington, Virginia. She was eighty-five years old.

Grace's favorite saying to young people was "A ship in port is safe, but that is not what ships are built for." Grace Hopper was not afraid to set sail—to take risks to accomplish her goals. That is why today Grace Murray Hopper is known as the Grandmother of the Computer Age, as Amazing Grace, and as the Grand Lady of Software.

Susan E. Clark
Saint Matthew Cathedral School
South Bend, Indiana

Suggested Reading

Billings, Charlene W. *Grace Hopper: Navy Admiral and Computer Pioneer.* Hillside, N.J.: Enslow Publishers, 1989.

Grinstein, Louise S., and Paul J. Campbell, eds. *Women of Mathematics: A Biobibliographic Sourcebook.* Westport, Conn.: Greenwood Press, 1987.

Julia Bowman Robinson

—With Every Candle, a Wish to Solve the "Tenth"

The "flapper era" was in full bloom. It was the Roaring Twenties. Prohibition had begun, and the woman-suffrage movement was in high gear. Silent movies were the rage, and big-time radio broadcasting brought entertainment into the home. The first commercial airplanes flew. Industries cranked out consumer products. As a result of World War I, the policies of isolationism were in effect. The despicable activities of the Ku Klux Klan accelerated. There were pockets of tremendous wealth in our country, and others that were filled with poverty and despair. These events and issues were at center stage in the lives of most Americans when Julia Bowman celebrated her third birthday on 8 December 1922.

These events, however, were not being noticed by Julia Bowman or her sister Constance, two years her senior. Their mother had just died, and their father was moving his little girls and their nurse from their Saint Louis, Missouri, home to Arizona to live with their grandmother. Mr. Bowman was staying behind to continue running his machine tool and equipment company.

Julia's grandmother lived in the middle of the desert near Camelback Mountain, twelve miles from Phoenix, in a quiet, primitive setting. Four families made up the entire community. Some of Julia's earliest childhood memories were of the hours she spent counting and arranging pebbles near a giant saguaro cactus within view of the mountains and her new Arizona home. In later years, as an accomplished mathematician, Julia recognized a link between her childhood love for counting and arranging pebbles and her love of counting theory and natural numbers. Knowing that what she proved about numbers would be true in any universe gave Julia a feeling of participating in the discovery of universal truths.

With his wife gone and his children more than a thousand miles away, Ralph Bowman was very much alone. Running his business grew wearisome. Within a year of his family's departure, he met and married a schoolteacher named Edenia Kridelbaugh. He sold his business and invested the money in ventures that he hoped would support his family for a lifetime. Then he and his new wife joined his daughters in Arizona.

Edenia quickly became a loving mother to Ralph's little girls. She cared for and taught them as her own. Edenia had taught many young girls before her marriage, but she thought Julia was probably the most stubborn child she had ever encountered. As an adult, Julia partially credited her success as a professional mathematician to that quality of stubborn perseverance.

In 1925, at Edenia's insistence and for the sake of the girls' education, the family left the remote Arizona settlement and moved to Point Loma on San Diego Bay. Their new home was much more densely populated, but like the desert, it was a place of adventure, exploration, and fanciful play. The girls' first school consisted of multigrade classrooms. Both girls completed more than one year of work during a school term, making them the youngest in their respective classes as they went through school.

On Easter Sunday in 1928, during the family's first year in Point Loma, a new little sister, Billie, was born. Billie was less than a year old when Julia contracted scarlet fever. Scarlet fever was a dangerous, highly infectious disease at that time. Julia's care included bed rest and isolation from others. Her father, trying to keep the disease from spreading (particularly to the baby), exclusively took over Julia's care. After a month, when Julia had recovered, the family celebrated by attending their first talking movie.

However, Julia was soon ill again with a more serious disease that sometimes accompanies scarlet fever—rheumatic fever. This time she had to stay in bed for a year in the home of a practical nurse. Too ill to do anything but rest and wait to recover, Julia became obsessed with a dream to own and ride a bicycle. (She was finally able to live this dream to its fullest in her late forties. In those years she could often be found riding over much of the United States or Holland on one of the many precision, custom-built bicycles from her personal collection.)

When Julia was well enough to return home from her stay with the nurse, her family moved to a neighboring community in San Diego. They moved primarily because Julia's parents did not want her to have to experience being behind her old classmates when she was able to return to school. During her second year of confinement, Julia was again able to be at home with her family. She was also well enough to have home schooling. Her father hired a teacher to work privately with Julia three mornings a week. In a year Julia had completed the state-required material for the fifth through the eighth grades of school. Obviously, the move to the new town had not been necessary to keep Julia from lagging behind her classmates.

In fall 1932, at age twelve, Julia entered the ninth grade at Theodore Roosevelt Junior High School. Many factors—having been isolated from other students for two years, being in a completely new student body, being younger than the other students in her class, and being a shy person by nature—contributed to a difficult entry into ninth grade for Julia. She remembered this period as a time when she made many stupid and embarrassing mistakes. She always felt alone and ate her lunch in the corner—quickly—so no one would notice that she was friendless. Many mathematicians and scientists seem to have spent periods of time in isolation as Julia did during her childhood. Perhaps these times can teach people patience and perseverance. Both these character traits are commonly found in scientists and mathematicians.

Julia finally found a friend, a warm and very artistically talented girl named Virginia Bell. Virginia reached out to Julia and invited her to eat lunch with her. Virginia remained Julia's best and only friend throughout high school. That she had only one close friend alarmed Julia's parents, but it did not seem to bother Julia.

During the ninth through twelfth grades, Julia continued to blossom into a student of promise. But not all academic subjects were easy for her. English was particularly troublesome. She was a slow reader and as a result, often found testing difficult. Two very competent women were among her mathematics teachers. Julia found that she had a love for both mathematics and science; she was the only girl in the school enrolled in physics.

Even though she was a shy person, Julia had a great deal of self-esteem, which she credited to her parents, and she was not concerned about what other people thought of her. Since it was very rare to see a girl in an upper-level mathematics or science course in her high school, that solid belief in herself no doubt contributed greatly to her success in both areas. She was an excellent mathematics and science student. She was also an outstanding achiever in mathematics and science competitions in and outside her school and state. Julia took a normal interest in many traditionally feminine teenage pursuits. She was interested in the boys in her classes. They, however, seemed to think of her primarily as a source of hints and answers to the mathematics problems they could not solve.

Julia's interests were not limited to mathematics and science. She was an accomplished horseback rider and an avid baseball fan, attending games and keeping detailed scores. She spent much of her allowance on sports magazines. She could also shoot a rifle and a pistol well, and she enjoyed perspective drawing.

Julia looked back on her high school years as a relaxed time. She did not feel pressured to be a great success or to go on to an impressive college. She knew she would attend college, but girls of this time usually went to a local college and became either teachers or nurses. Julia's parents and teachers did not seem to expect anything different from her. At graduation, when Julia walked off with many awards, her mother jokingly asked her, "What are we going to do with a girl like you?" Julia's father responded (as he gave his daughter her graduation present, a very expensive slide rule for making very close approximations of elaborate calculations in scientific and mathematics problems), "Oh, she will just have to marry her math professor in college!"

Julia's mother felt strongly that a girl should be educated so that she could support herself in a useful occupation. Julia enrolled at San Diego State University, where her older sister, Constance, was already attending. Julia assumed that she would become a teacher. Only a few highly educated staff members were on the faculty at San Diego State. In her first year of college, this situation did not seriously concern Julia. But as her major in mathematics required higher-level mathematics, Julia began to view the school's lack of highly educated and trained teachers as a distinct shortcoming. She wanted to transfer to the University of California at Los Angeles (UCLA) or some other highly accredited school.

In 1936, as Julia's sophomore year in college unfolded, the United States was falling deeper into a depression. The economic turmoil of the Great Depression had not passed her family by. All the money Ralph Bowman had so confidently invested in 1923 from the sale of his company had been wiped out. Like many other men and women in financial despair during those dark days in the 1930s, Ralph Bowman took his life.

The family moved to a small apartment. An aunt who was a schoolteacher in Saint Louis was able to give the Bowmans some financial help, and in spite of the hardship, both girls were able to remain in their local college that year. After Constance graduated and received a short period of advanced training at the University of California at Berkeley, she found a good teaching job and was also able to help support the family.

Julia's interest in mathematics continued to grow, and her dream to be in a truly enriched mathematics atmosphere became a passion. She wanted to go to a school that had a "real" mathematics department. She had already taken all the courses offered at her local college. The school was planning to start an honors program the following year, with Julia as its only star student, but this program did not fulfill her needs. With Constance able to add to the family income, Julia headed off to Berkeley for her senior year of college. She chose Berkeley instead of UCLA at the suggestion of a new teacher who had just joined the staff of San Diego State. The strength of Berkeley's mathematics program and the composition of its mathematics faculty were the deciding factors.

Julia had always planned to get a teacher's degree in order to teach mathematics in high school, as her mother had expected her to do. But a new push to attract male teachers to secondary education, particularly in the fields of mathematics and science, made it doubtful whether Julia would be able to find a job after graduation. In light of this situation, she took five courses in mathematics her first year at Berkeley and began to explore ways other than teaching to use her mathematics education.

One of the courses Julia was enrolled in her first year at Berkeley was on number theory. By the second semester, only four students remained in the class; Julia was the only woman. The instructor, Raphael M. Robinson, took a special interest in Julia. He often asked her to accompany him on long walks after class, discussing mathematics and getting to know her.

Julia believed she was living a fairy tale come true. She suddenly was part of a world in which both the students and the staff loved mathematics as much as she did. At Berkeley many social events revolved around the students' and faculty's common interest in mathematics. Julia was at home among her colleagues, and her confidence in herself and in her knowledge of mathematics abounded. She perceived herself as an ugly duckling turned into a swan. She was also changing from a caged parakeet with clipped wings to an eagle learning to soar with the strongest and best of her kind.

The person who had the greatest impact on Julia's life, both mathematically and personally, was Professor Raphael Robinson. Raphael helped her advance her mathematics skills and love of mathematics as radically at the college level as her home-schooling teacher had helped her advance her education as a child. Raphael fell in love with Julia and she with him; they were married a few weeks after the United States entered World War II. Julia always felt that her success as a woman in mathematics hinged to a great extent on being able to walk through doors in the professional mathematics world that at that time could be opened only by a man. Raphael opened those doors for Julia and allowed her to walk into a world most women could not enter. She had access to the professional society and facilities needed for professional growth. Once inside those doors, she proved herself to be a worthy guest in the house.

Julia's early work as a graduate student was in statistics. Although she found statistics messy and not as beautiful and pleasing as pure number theory, her first published work was in this field. Because of a rule at Berkeley forbidding the spouse of a faculty member to teach concurrently in the same department, Julia had to give up her graduate teaching fellowship. Julia and Raphael had planned to have a family, and this interruption in her professional life seemed to offer an appropriate opportunity.

Julia continued to audit mathematics classes but also enjoyed spending her time shopping and decorating her new home. She was delighted to discover that she was pregnant but was devastated a few months later when she miscarried. She then found out that because of her childhood illness, scar tissue had built up around her heart, leaving her unable to endure the physical strain of bearing a child. The doctors also feared that her heart problems would shorten her life and told her she should not expect to live past forty. (Almost twenty years later, when Julia was forty-one, newly developed surgical techniques were used to repair Julia's heart, allowing her to enjoy the health and vitality she had not known since early childhood. During this time she became an avid bicyclist.)

As Julia recovered from the grief of the loss of her child and the knowledge that she was not able to have a family of her own, Raphael encouraged her to get more actively involved in mathematics. She and Raphael both worked on recursion formulas while on leave at Princeton the following year. Julia worked hard. Her results were published at the end of that year, 1947.

During the early months of World War II, Alfred Tarski, a Polish mathematician specializing in logic, came from Poland to be a visiting lecturer at Harvard. Before he was scheduled to return home, Germany invaded Poland. Tarski was unable to return to his homeland, and he had no permanent position in the United States. He ended up at Berkeley and became a valuable addition to the staff. He was known as one of the greatest logicians in the world. When Julia returned to Berkeley after her year with Raphael at Princeton, she started to work toward her Ph.D. with Alfred Tarski as her advisor.

Doctoral students are given a topic to research and to which they can contribute new insights and information. In mathematics this topic is often a mathematical proof or problem that no one has been able to solve. The problem in rational algebra that Julia was originally assigned by Tarski did not particularly interest her. Julia later expressed her opinion that perhaps graduate students would more readily persevere in attaining their doctorates if the topics for their doctoral theses were selected *for* or *by* them with more care.

The actual topic of Julia's doctoral thesis was suggested at a luncheon discussion between Tarski and Raphael at the Men's Faculty Club. In those days women were not allowed in the club for lunch, but Raphael related the discussion to Julia when he returned home. The problem that particularly interested her was in the area that is often considered her main field—the borderline between logic and number theory. When she presented her work to Tarski, he was delighted. Tarski was an inspiring teacher. His students left his lectures knowing that mathematics was not a finished discipline. The types of problems he presented made clear to his students that much progress could still be made in mathematics and that they could contribute to the field. With her doctorate completed, Julia began work on one of those problems in 1948. The solution to that problem, known as "Hilbert's tenth," was to be her major contribution to mathematics and would not be completed until 1970.

In 1949 Julia worked for the Rand Corporation. During that year Rand offered prize money to anyone who could prove any one of several problems in game theory. A game was to be set up between two fictitious players. Players alternately were to make the best choice of the moves available. This process was to be carried out indefinitely. The question was, Would the play always produce a winner? Julia successfully proved that it would, and her results were published in 1951. The theorem presented in that paper has been called the most important theorem in elementary game theory. She did not, however, receive the prize money because she was an employee of the firm.

During the 1950s Julia experienced her most embarrassing failure. She got involved in research on hydrodynamics at Stanford University. She realized later that although she worked very hard, she was out of her field and should never have taken the job. She was unable to prove anything. She resigned without even turning in a report.

Soon after, a magazine article on Adlai Stevenson (then governor of Illinois) caught her attention. Julia became active in politics. She spent her talent and most of her time campaigning for Stevenson and several other Democratic candidates from 1952 to 1958.

During those years of campaigning, Julia never abandoned her work on Hilbert's tenth problem. David Hilbert, known as the foremost mathematician in 1900, had composed a list of twenty-three major problems. Of these, many have not yet been solved. The tenth problem is "Given a Diophantine [only integer solutions] equation with any number of unknown quantities and with rational integral numerical coefficients [and whole-number exponents]: to devise a process according to which it can be determined by a finite number of operations whether the equation is solvable in rational integers." For example, $x^2 + y^2 - 2 = 0$ has four Diophantine solutions, (1, 1), (−1, 1), (−1, −1), (1, −1), but $x^2 + y^2 - 3 = 0$ has none.

Throughout the 1960s, after her open-heart surgery, Julia continued to work on Hilbert's tenth problem. She was beginning to become rather discouraged. Years later, after she had found the solution, she revealed that year after year when she blew out her birthday candles, she had wished that someone would find the solution. Finally, in February 1970 a friend phoned to tell her that a young Russian mathematician in Leningrad had solved the part of Hilbert's tenth that she had been unable to solve. This solution was all that was needed to complete Julia's proof. Young Yuri Matijasevich, only twenty-two years old, had constructed the missing part of the proof, using Fibonacci numbers—a series that has been known since the thirteenth century. His proof contained ideas that would have been included in an elementary number-theory course!

As Julia blew out the candles on her fifty-first birthday cake, she realized that she needed a new wish. In 1971 Julia visited with Yuri Matijasevich in Russia. She commented that when she was starting work on Hilbert's tenth, he was still an infant. She had to wait for him to grow up to help her out. Both mathematicians received much acclaim as a result of their combined success. At the time of her visit, Julia Bowman Robinson was regarded in the Soviet Union as the second most famous Robinson, Robinson Crusoe being the first.

After solving Hilbert's problem, in 1975 Julia became the first female mathematician to be elected to the National Academy of Sciences; she modestly claimed that other women were more deserving. She was also made a full professor at Berkeley, even though her health would not allow her to carry a full-time class load. In 1982 she was the first woman nominated for the presidency of the American Mathematical Society (AMS). Raphael did not want her to accept. He wanted her to conserve her energy for mathematical research. Julia decided that as a woman and a mathematician she had no alternative but to accept. She wanted to do everything that she could to encourage women to become mathematicians.

Julia received many other honors, including election to the American Academy of Arts and Sciences, an honorary degree from Smith College, and a sixty-thousand-dollar-a-year grant (for five consecutive years) from the MacArthur Foundation to conduct mathematics research. Julia was also featured in *Vogue*, the *Village Voice*, and the *Ladies Home Journal* as one of the one hundred most outstanding women in America. Julia's response (Reid 1986, p. 21) was, "All this attention has been gratifying but also embarrassing. What I really am is a mathematician. Rather than being remembered as the first woman this or that, I would prefer to be remembered, as a mathematician should, simply for the theorems I have proved and problems I have solved."

The needs and concerns of the American Mathematical Society occupied Julia for a full ten years. She also frequently worked during this time on problems of human rights. In 1984 at the summer meeting of the AMS, over which she was presiding, Julia discovered that she was suffering from leukemia. She died the following summer on 30 July 1985.

Julia Robinson was born in 1919 at a time when being a girl or a woman in mathematics was different from being one today. Today you are likely to have more than one girl in your mathematics classes in high school or college. People will not find it strange to work with a female mathematician. Now female mathematicians are common and welcomed in secondary school and university mathematics departments, and they hold respected positions in industry and in research. Women in mathematics live full, rewarding lives, centering on mathematics and reaching out into many other fields of accomplishment and enrichment. Mathematics in the twenty-first century will be one of the world's most needed, most challenging, and most rewarding fields. Female mathematicians will be on the cutting edge of research, technological advancement, and industrial application. Thanks to women like Julia Bowman Robinson, the doors leading to exciting careers in mathematics have been opened for women everywhere.

Joan Fisher Koppy
Elkhart Central High School
Elkhart, Indiana

Suggested Reading

Albers, Donald J., and Gerald L. Alexanderson. *Mathematical People: Profiles and Interviews*. Boston: Birkhäuser Boston, 1985.

Grinstein, Louise S., and Paul J. Campbell, eds. *Women of Mathematics: A Biobibliographic Sourcebook*. Westport, Conn.: Greenwood Press, 1987.

"Hilbert's Tenth Problem." *Scientific American*, November 1973, pp. 84–91.

Reid, Constance. "The Autobiography of Julia Robinson." *College Mathematics* 17 (January 1986): 2–21.

Rosalyn Sussman Yalow

—Scientist without Boundaries

Careers in science are dominated by men. How can a woman overcome the obstacles that hinder her from being successful in this field? Rosalyn Yalow's life shows that a talented woman can fulfill her dreams by embracing opportunities to exhibit her abilities. Even though her parents had not continued their education beyond elementary school, Rosalyn resolved to become educated. Her determination led her to become a pioneer in biochemistry at a time when society's stereotypes indicated that women were best suited for clerical work.

Rosalyn Sussman was born 19 July 1921. Her parents, Simon and Clara, owned a small twine and paper business. Although they were not highly educated, they encouraged Rosalyn to do well in school and praised her efforts. They dreamed that their daughter would someday become a teacher—a highly respected career choice for women at that time. Little did they realize that this talented young girl from Albany, New York, would become the second woman to earn the Nobel Prize in medicine.

The path to attaining this prize began at Hunter College, where Rosalyn earned a bachelor of arts in chemistry and physics in 1941. Graduating with honors, Rosalyn went on to study in the College of Engineering at the University of Illinois and work as a teaching assistant. She was the only female in a class of 400 students. She persevered until she earned a Ph.D. in physics—at the time, a rare accomplishment for a woman.

Rosalyn met Aaron Yalow on her first day of classes at the University of Illinois. They were married in 1943.

During the early 1940s, at the beginning of World War II, much research was being done in nuclear physics. Rosalyn was involved in researching radioactive substances while working on her degree at the University of Illinois. This field of study became the focus of her life's work. Rosalyn's achievements blazed a trail that opened this field of scientific research to other women. Her parents must have been proud to see that their daughter's success went far beyond their dreams for her. She became a teacher of physics and pre-engineering as well as a research scientist.

After earning her doctorate, Rosalyn continued her work with radioactive substances, that is, elements that have an atomic number above 83. Some are found in nature, and some are compounded in the laboratory. The creation of the atomic bomb is an example of the scientific use of radioactive elements—albeit a potentially destructive use.

Rosalyn's research contributed to saving lives. She developed a method to measure the amount of protein in the blood. Protein reacts in certain ways with radioactive substances. This reaction is called *radioimmunoassay* (RIA). Rosalyn was gifted in developing methods of measuring radioactive substances. Marking substances with radioisotopes allows them to be traced as they follow a path through body tissue. A machine much like a Geiger counter was used in this process.

Rosalyn's appetite for discovery became greater with each new investigation. She was a hard worker and was generous with her knowledge. Rosalyn's expertise in physics was combined with Solomon A. Berson's expertise in the chemistry of the human body. These two researchers worked together for more than twenty years, developing ways to track diseases and body chemicals. One disease they focused on was diabetes. Rosalyn was not discouraged when other scientists rejected their theory that the body makes antibodies against insulin. She knew that new ideas are often not widely accepted immediately. It's a long, hard process. Rosalyn Yalow was not afraid to work through this process.

Rosalyn's independent research has helped the scientific community make strides in testing for diabetes, reproductive failure, drug abuse, and growth disorders. Her research has led to methods of measuring the levels of the substances that allow nerve impulses to be transmitted across the gap between nerve cells. She also has contributed to the screening of many different viruses in the blood of donors. She has also used RIA to track leukemia viruses in the early stages of the disease before tumors start growing.

Albert Einstein once said that imagination is more important than knowledge. Through hard work, Rosalyn Yalow built a strong base of knowledge that stimulated her imagination, and she discovered new information that could be used to educate and help others. In her Nobel lecture she said, "The first telescopes opened the heavens; the first microscope opened the world of microbes" (Wasson 1987, p. 1150). Rosalyn believed that the use of radioactive materials would open up new avenues in science and medicine.

Rosalyn Yalow's contributions to the world of science, medicine, and education have not gone unnoticed. A recipient of the Nobel Prize in 1977, Rosalyn has also earned thirty-five other prestigious awards. She has received many fellowships and has been recognized with distinguished professorships. She has also chaired the clinical science department of a hospital, and she has assumed four different directorships. Both Saint

Mary's College in Notre Dame, Indiana, and Indiana University awarded her honorary doctor of science degrees in 1983.

The numerous awards Rosalyn Yalow has received were well earned. She gained self-confidence through hard work and determination. Rosalyn developed a sense of self-worth by pursuing a task with enthusiasm and by refusing to give up. Her many positions helped her create a base of knowledge on which she could build. She did not choose to learn only those things she felt were important. She did not divorce herself from other fields of science by focusing on only one. She found special ways to integrate her scientific interests with other sciences. The techniques of one discipline helped her solve problems in another field.

Having been married for more than forty years and having reared two children during that time, Rosalyn has been a shining example to women. She has succeeded in a profession dominated by men. Much of Rosalyn's collaboration with men occurred at a time when men received most of the credit for research and scientific success. Following the death of Solomon Berson, her research partner, the scientific community thought that Rosalyn's work would end, because their colleagues believed that Solomon was the "brains" of the team. Five years later, she received the Nobel Prize.

Rosalyn's perception of the importance of monetary rewards for her work is worth noting. Throughout her career, attaining wealth was never her goal. Her RIA testing equipment brought large profits to drug companies, yet she and her partner had no desire to patent the equipment that would one day be enormously valuable to the field of medicine. She worked primarily to improve the quality of the lives of others. Rosalyn believed, however, that as the equal of men, she had an equal right to the fruits of her labors. When she was awarded the Nobel Prize, she made certain that the Nobel committee emphasized the importance of her contributions—not simply for her sake but for the sake of all women. She wanted to compete and be recognized on equal terms with men, even refusing recognition by the *Ladies Home Journal* because it implied that her work was remarkable *for a woman*. Rosalyn thought her work was remarkable for either a man *or* a woman.

Rosalyn Yalow has worked independently and with others to make new discoveries in scientific research. Rosalyn defines science as "a result of investigations." She is her own person who believes in and loves her work and is challenged by the possibility of new revelations.

Receiving many awards, especially the Nobel Prize, has been gratifying for her. However, she finds her biggest thrill in the science laboratory, pursuing knowledge no one has yet brought to light. The dream of new discovery keeps Rosalyn Yalow motivated to search and investigate, to question and solve problems, to discover and invent.

Judith Munson
Kesling Middle School
LaPorte, Indiana

Suggested Reading

Dash, Joan. *The Triumph of Discovery: Women Scientists Who Won the Nobel Prize.* Englewood Cliffs, N.J.: Julian Messner, 1991.

DeBruin, Jerry. *Scientists around the World.* Carthage, Ill.: Good Apple, 1987.

Wasson, Tyler, ed. *Nobel Prize Winners: An H. W. Wilson Biographical Dictionary.* New York: H. W. Wilson Co., 1987.

Evelyn Boyd Granville

—African American Pioneer

In 1945 Evelyn Boyd Granville had just graduated from Smith College summa cum laude (with highest honors). This was a major accomplishment for a black woman in our society. She and others in her family had put in many long hours in order to make it possible; now she was on her way to Yale University to continue her graduate work. Evelyn had attended the racially segregated public schools of Washington, D.C., and had graduated from a private women's college, but she was not quite sure what the future would hold for her.

Evelyn was born 1 May 1924 to William Boyd and Julia Walker Boyd in Washington, D.C. Her older sister, Doris, was about twenty-two months old at the time of Evelyn's birth. Evelyn's father left the family early in her childhood. The girls were reared by their mother and their mother's twin sister, Louise Walker.

Both Evelyn's mother and Louise had high school diplomas. Louise had graduated from Miner Normal Teachers College with a kindergarten teacher's certificate. Instead of teaching, Louise chose to work with her sister Julia for the United States Bureau of Engraving and Printing. They worked as examiners for over thirty-five years. Their devotion and hard work greatly influenced Evelyn's educational goals and desires.

Evelyn's sister, Doris, graduated from high school and entered college. In 1942 she left college to establish a career as a statistical assistant in the United States Census Bureau.

Evelyn spent her high school years in the public schools of Washington, D.C. Although Dunbar High School was racially segregated, it maintained a high academic standard and was known as an institution of excellence. Evelyn's teachers were superior role models. They included Mary Cromwell, a University of Pennsylvania graduate, and Evelyn's mathematics teacher, Ulysses Basset, a graduate of Yale. Because of Evelyn's high academic standing, these fine teachers encouraged her to apply to some of the best colleges in the United States.

Evelyn chose Smith College, a private college for women in Northampton, Massachusetts, where she was able to obtain a partial scholarship. She spent her summers working for the National Bureau of Standards in Washington to help pay for part of her college education. Her mother and aunt helped her pay for the rest, oftentimes making great sacrifices to do so.

While at Smith College, Evelyn studied astronomy. She thoroughly enjoyed the subject and was interested in becoming an astronomer. In those days, astronomers had to live in the great observatories, which were frequently totally isolated. Evelyn knew that she would not be happy in that situation. Later on in life, Evelyn reflected that if she had possessed the ability to see into the future, she might have foreseen the growth of the space program and continued her studies in astronomy. Instead, she decided to study mathematics with Professors Neal McCoy and Susan Rambo.

In 1945 few women were graduating in the area of mathematics, and black women in mathematics were even fewer. But Evelyn was not finished with her academic career. She won awards for graduate study from Yale University. In her first year the awards were supplemented by a fellowship from Smith College. She received her doctorate at Yale University in 1949 under Einar Hille, a leading mathematician of the time. Hille had served a term as president of the American Mathematical Society and was a member of the National Academy of Science. At the same time another African American woman, Marjorie Lee Browne, received her doctorate in mathematics from the University of Michigan. Evelyn Boyd Granville and Marjorie Lee Browne were the first black women to receive doctorates in mathematics. Not until ten years later did the third African American woman earn a doctorate in mathematics.

After completing her doctorate, Evelyn went to New York University to continue her research. She enjoyed the academic life and decided to apply for a teaching position. Evelyn had several interviews, including one at a nearby college. One faculty member reported that when the hiring committee discovered that Evelyn was black, they laughed at her application and would not consider her for the job. Another faculty member reported that it was not her race that was the problem but her gender. Regardless of whether racial or sexual discrimination was involved, these practices were common barriers that an African American woman had to overcome. Evelyn was not aware that her race and gender were factors in her interview until many years later.

Despite the common attitudes of discrimination, Evelyn obtained a teaching position at Fisk University, a private college in Nashville, Tennessee. Fisk was established as a college for black students but has always accepted students regardless of race. Evelyn's appointment at Fisk coincided with the appointment of Lee Lorch as the new chair of the Department of Mathematics. Lorch is a white mathematician who encouraged Evelyn in the pursuit of a mathematics career at a time when a career in mathematics was considered unacceptable or unattainable for African Americans—particularly for black women. In those days African American students were encouraged to prepare for careers in the ministry, the health professions, or public school teaching.

Evelyn taught at Fisk for only two years, but in that short time she was able to inspire several of her students. Two of her students, Vivienne Malone Mayes and Etta Zuber Falconer, followed in Evelyn's footsteps and received doctorates in mathematics.

In 1952 Evelyn left Fisk University and found employment with the Diamond Ordnance Fuze Laboratories of the United States Army. Her job involved working with the engineers and scientists who were developing missile fuzes. She helped them solve the mathematical problems they encountered in the project.

Evelyn's love for astronomy resurfaced and attracted her to her next job. In 1956 she was hired by International Business Machines (IBM) to work on the Project Vanguard and Project Mercury space probes. She helped calculate the orbits and helped design the computer procedures for the probes. She also programmed the IBM 650 and 704 computers.

In 1961–62 she continued her research on orbit calculations. While at the U.S. Space Technology Laboratories in 1963, Evelyn worked on the Apollo Project. In 1960 Evelyn had married the Reverend Gamaliel Mansfield Collins, whose three children occasionally lived with them. The marriage ended in divorce seven years later.

Evelyn became a full professor at California State University in Los Angeles in 1967. She worked with the State of California Miller Mathematics Improvement Program. In this position Evelyn was able to expand her experience by teaching part-time in a nearby elementary school. She also directed an after-school program designed for the enrichment of children in kindergarten through fifth grade. During this time she and noted mathematician Jason Frand coauthored *Theory and Application of Mathematics for Teachers*. It was published in 1975 and widely used at many colleges and universities.

In 1970 Evelyn married Edward V. Granville, a real estate broker, whom she met while she was teaching at California State University in Los Angeles. He had two grown daughters.

After spending seventeen years teaching at California State University in Los Angeles, Evelyn Granville retired at the age of sixty. She and her husband purchased a sixteen-acre farm in Texas that boasted eight hundred chickens. Evelyn and Edward soon went into the business of selling eggs. But before long Evelyn missed teaching. She resumed her teaching career full-time in the mathematics and computer science department at Texas College in Tyler. She is currently a visiting professor at the University of Texas at Tyler and uses the farm as a pleasant diversion.

When asked about balancing her personal life and her career, Evelyn responded, "I never encountered any problems in combining career and private life. Black women have always had to work" (Grinstein and Campbell 1987, p. 59). Evelyn has no children, which may have made it easier for her to pursue her career. African American women, she says, are brought up expecting to be required to work outside the home. Thus, she believes, many black women do not experience the conflict of career and family that many white women struggle with.

In looking back over her life, Evelyn wrote, "I feel that I have had a very rich life. I have been blessed with a fine family, an excellent education, many friends that I have gathered over the years, and last, but by no means least, a happy (second) marriage" (Grinstein and Campbell 1987, p. 59).

Evelyn Boyd Granville is known as a distinguished researcher, teacher, and author. She was one of the first two black women to receive a doctorate in mathematics at a time when very few women of any race even considered entering this field. She has led a very fulfilling life and has opened the doors for other women to enter the world of mathematics.

Joan G. Tetzlaff
Navarre Middle School
South Bend, Indiana

Suggested Reading

Grinstein, Louise S., and Paul J. Campbell, eds. *Women of Mathematics: A Biobiblio-graphic Sourcebook*. Westport, Conn.: Greenwood Press, 1987.

Kenschaft, Patricia. "Black Men and Women in Mathematical Research." *Journal of Black Studies* 18 (December 1987): 170–90.

———. "Black Women in Mathematics in the United States." *American Mathematical Monthly* 88 (August 1981): 592–604.

Mayes, Vivienne M. "Lee Lorch at Fisk: A Tribute." *American Mathematical Monthly.* 83 (November 1976): 709–11.

Perl, Teri H., and Joan M. Manning. *Women, Numbers, and Dreams*. Santa Rosa, Calif.: National Women's History Project, 1982.

Mary Ellen Estill Rudin

—Mathematics for the Fun of It

Being young and adventurous was a challenge in the town of Leakey, Texas, in the early 1930s. The access to this small town was a fifty-mile-long dirt road. The surroundings were simple. The people, too, were simple. The school was the center of activity in the town. The children had few toys to play with, a limited number of books to read, and not many sources of entertainment besides the radio. They rode to school on horseback. Most families had no running water and little money for extras. How did the children spend their time? What did they do? How did they have fun?

Mary Ellen Estill was born in Hillsboro, Texas, on 7 December 1924, but she grew up in this environment, which may have contributed to making her a confident and creative mathematician. She made the most of these substandard conditions. She used her time "just to think." Games were not purchased; they were invented. Mary Ellen herself said that using the imagination "contributes to the making of a mathematician—having some time to think and being in the habit of imagining all sorts of complicated things" (Albers, Alexanderson, and Reid 1990, p. 286).

Mary Ellen was left to do things on her own most of the time. Her only brother was ten years younger than she, so their relationship was not close. She thought of him more as a nephew or a son than as a brother.

Both of Mary Ellen's parents came from middle-class families. Joe Jefferson Estill was a civil engineer. The family moved to Leakey because of Mr. Estill's work. He had been hired to modernize the dirt road that led out of their little town, but because of the Great Depression, funds were never allocated to complete the road. Mr. Estill had a degree in civil engineering from the University of Texas. Irene Shook Estill had graduated with a bachelor of arts degree and used it to teach high school English.

Mary Ellen's parents set expectations for her early in her life. Her mother wanted Mary Ellen to do what she liked, but she expected her to support herself. Her parents often encouraged her, so her self-confidence was high. She is quoted as having said, "Having failed five thousand times doesn't seem to make me any less confident. At least I don't feel bound by any serious constraints or doubts about my ability" (Albers, Alexanderson, and Reid 1990, p. 289).

Greatly influenced by her parents' emphasis on education, Mary Ellen claimed that she had always known she was going to go to a university. Her father encouraged her choice of the University of Texas. He thought his alma mater was a superior school. He even accompanied her to registration to help pick out her classes. That registration day turned out to be a turning point in Mary Ellen's life.

Mary Ellen had loved many of the subjects in high school. She liked not only mathematics but history, English, physics, philosophy, and Spanish as well. She had never expected to choose mathematics as a career. She had been advised by her father, among others, to sign up for a liberal arts program. She was planning to take a variety of courses to find out what she was interested in and to see where her talents lay. When she got to the registration site, she became overwhelmed. A lot of people were in line at the liberal arts table, but only a few students stood at the mathematics table. Mary Ellen decided to check out what the mathematics department had to offer. The man who was assisting the students had a discussion with her. He asked her all sorts of questions that involved logic, and he helped her choose her classes. One of them was a mathematics class.

The next day Mary Ellen went to mathematics class and discovered that the man who had assisted her at registration was her professor, R. L. Moore. Professor Moore was well known for his research *and* his teaching. He taught Mary Ellen mathematics—including trigonometry, analytic geometry, and calculus—throughout her college years. She learned to do independent research because R. L. Moore's style of teaching encouraged such exploration.

Mary Ellen thought of herself as the one student who always had the right answer in the back of her mind. She would watch Professor Moore question the other students, and time after time, they would give incorrect answers. Finally, he would call on her, knowing she had the answer he was looking for. Although she did not particularly like Professor Moore's style of teaching, it definitely helped build her confidence.

Mary Ellen graduated in 1944 with a bachelor of arts degree. She had spent only three years at her undergraduate studies because the involvement of the United States in World War II forced changes in the school schedules.

Professor Moore thought it important for Mary Ellen to go on to graduate school. He had previously had two female students whom he advised to continue to do research after they graduated, but one went on to teach and the other became a missionary—pursuits he thought wasted their talents. Although many of Professor Moore's male students did not go on to do research, he was more distressed when the women decided not to continue their studies in graduate school. He made Mary Ellen aware of his concern and told her that she could not be another "failure."

Mary Ellen did decide to do graduate work. She stayed at the University of Texas with R. L. Moore as her adviser. She was not entirely happy, however, with the education she received. R. L. Moore conducted the course so that all the students worked independently. When they got together for class, they sometimes discussed their research, but most of the time they talked about unrelated matters. Mary Ellen felt cheated. After she received her doctorate, she claimed that she had never really learned some of the important elements of mathematics, such as algebra and analysis. Moore stressed the development of his students' confidence and capabilities more than he stressed "textbook" mathematics, much to Mary Ellen's regret.

Professor Moore helped Mary Ellen get her first job at Duke University, where she taught until 1953. During this time, she met and began dating Walter Rudin.

Walter was an Austrian who had attended school in Switzerland. He moved to France and eventually came to visit the United States. His sister was in graduate school at Duke University. Although Walter had never gone to college, he convinced Duke University to enroll him as a junior in the mathematics department.

At times during their courtship, Walter wanted to get married but Mary Ellen did not. At other times, she wanted to marry but he did not. Finally they were both ready.

After their wedding in 1953, the Rudins moved to Rochester, New York, where Walter had accepted a position on the faculty at the University of Rochester. Mary Ellen was jobless, but that situation did not concern her; she was happy just being married to Walter.

As at other times in her life, Mary Ellen was given an opportunity without seeking it. When she arrived at the University of Rochester with her husband, the mathematics department asked her to teach a calculus class. Despite having only a part-time position, Mary Ellen was not worried about finances because Walter had a full-time teaching job. She taught simply for the fun of it. She loved being married as much as she loved working with mathematics.

Walter and Mary Ellen Rudin had four children: Catherine, Eleanor, Robert Jefferson, and Charles Michael. Mary Ellen loved to work on her mathematics while the children climbed around and on her. She enjoyed being in the midst of everything at once. When the children were young, it was easier to teach only half-time, but when the children were grown, Mary Ellen went back to full-time teaching.

Besides teaching, Mary Ellen Rudin did extensive research in mathematics. She developed a specialty in set-theoretic topology, which deals with sets and how they are related. She has written approximately seventy papers and books dealing with this subject. The titles include *Concerning Abstract Spaces*, *Directed Sets Which Converge*, *The Shrinkable Property*, and *Set-Theoretic Constructions of Non-Shrinkable Open Covers*.

Mary Ellen has received three research grants from the National Science Foundation. She is a member of the American Mathematical Society and the Association for Women in Mathematics. She is also a member of many national boards and has given many lectures throughout the country. She has won two major awards: the Prize of the Mathematical Society of the Netherlands and the Grace Chisholm Young Professorship at the University of Wisconsin.

Mary Ellen and Walter are both professors emeriti at the University of Wisconsin—Madison. Besides lecturing and writing, she is active in discovering and encouraging gifted young mathematicians in a statewide program.

Throughout her life, Mary Ellen Rudin has worked hard and has never lost confidence in herself. Commenting on women as mathematicians, Mary Ellen stated, "You just need stamina, and women often have a great deal of stamina" (Albers and Reid 1988, p. 136). Mary Ellen Rudin has had—and continues to have—what it takes to be a great woman of mathematics.

Linda Waltz
Saint Anthony de Padua School
South Bend, Indiana

Suggested Reading

Albers, Donald J., Gerald L. Alexanderson, and Constance Reid, eds. *More Mathematical People: Contemporary Conversations*. San Diego: Academic Press, 1990.

Albers, Donald J., and Constance Reid. "An Interview with Mary Ellen Rudin." *College Mathematics Journal* 2 (March 1988).

Grinstein, Louise S., and Paul J. Campbell, eds. *Women of Mathematics: A Biobibliographic Sourcebook*. Westport, Conn.: Greenwood Press, 1987.

Dian Fossey

—American Naturalist, Primatologist, Zoologist

20

Rwanda is a tiny central African state with a population of six million. The Virunga mountain range, consisting of eight volcanoes, is shared by Rwanda, Uganda, and Zaire. Two volcanic peaks, Mount Karisimbi and Mount Visoke, stretch up toward the sky. Nestled between these peaks, ten thousand feet up Visoke's slope above Lake Kivu, is the Karisoke Research Centre. This tranquil setting erupted in violence on 27 December 1985. Nyirmachabelli, the "Woman Who Lives Alone in the Forest," also known as Nyiramaribi, the "Woman Who Lives Alone on the Mountain," was found in her Karisoke hut with her face slashed in two by a panga (machete). Kanyaragana, the Rwandan who discovered her body, ran out of Dian Fossey's house screaming, "Dian kufa kufa" (Dian is dead). The mountain gorillas of Rwanda and Zaire had forever lost their friend and protector.

Dian Fossey was born in Louisville, Kentucky, in 1932 and was the daughter of George and Kitty Fossey. George enjoyed the outdoors and displayed a love and respect for living things. This aspect of his character had a profound effect on Dian and on her attitudes about nature. Dian's parents were divorced when she was six years old.

When Kitty remarried, Dian found her stepfather, Richard Price, to be stern and insensitive. He forbade her to have any pets. Dian was very secretive about her early years, but friends say she had a lonely, troubled childhood.

After graduating from high school, Dian attended Marin Junior College in 1949, and the following year she attempted a pre-veterinary-medicine program at the University of California. She eventually dropped out when she failed her physics and chemistry courses. In 1954 she received a degree in occupational therapy from San Jose State College and went on to work at the Kosair Crippled Children's Hospital in Louisville.

Dian was a shy person in an imposing six-foot-tall body. Those who knew her well appreciated her keen sense of humor. Dian's interest in Africa was first aroused by a reporter who had recently returned from that continent. Africa became Dian's dream. She was so determined to take an African safari that she borrowed the money at 24 percent interest to finance a trip. This seven-week adventure in 1963 surpassed her expectations. Her itinerary included Kenya, Tanganyika, Uganda, the Belgian Congo (now Zaire), and Southern Rhodesia (now Zimbabwe). She met the eminent anthropologist Dr. Louis Leakey and saw the mountain gorillas for the first time. After her return home, she continued to dream of Africa. Through friends she met Alexie Forrester, a Southern Rhodesian student attending the University of Notre Dame in South Bend, Indiana. He later became her fiancé, and during their courtship, he shared many stories about Africa with her.

In 1966, three years after her return to the United States, Dian met Dr. Leakey again, at a lecture in Louisville. He remembered her and was so impressed that he offered her the opportunity to study the mountain gorillas of Virunga. Dian accepted his offer and at his request, had her appendix removed as a precautionary measure because of the remoteness of the area. On 15 December 1966, she left her job, her home, and her fiancé. With funds provided by the National Geographic Society and the Wilkie Brothers Foundation, Dian spent the next eighteen years living on the slopes of a dormant volcano, studying mountain gorillas.

Dian initially began her work in Zaire on Mount Mikeno's slopes. Except for the appearance of a few African trackers, Dian spent her first year alone. After six months she was forced to leave Zaire because of the political turmoil in Kivu Province. Her new camp in Rwanda was five miles from the old camp and consisted of several sheet-metal cabins (her hut, the research assistants' or visitors' hut, a men's hut for trackers and the antipoaching patrol, and an open-sided hut for park guards). A rough jeep road came within two hundred feet of the research station, but the rest of the three-mile winding way had to be climbed on foot. The nearest store was nineteen miles away.

Alexie Forrester was concerned about Dian's safety and arrived in Africa in 1967 to persuade her to return home and become his wife. Dian refused, and the engagement ended. Africa became home to Dian, and the mountain gorillas became her closest friends.

Dian learned that there are three species of gorillas. *Gorilla gorilla gorilla* is the most numerous. These gorillas are found in the African rain forests in southeastern Nigeria and throughout Cameroon, Equatorial Guinea, the Congo, Zaire, Gabon, and all along the Congo River. *Gorilla gorilla graueri* is the eastern lowland gorilla, found eight hundred miles east in central Africa and Zaire. Dian studied the mountain gorilla species, *Gorilla gorilla beringei*, which inhabits the high volcanic slopes of the Virunga Mountains of Uganda, Rwanda, and Zaire. Gorillas have a deep barrel chest, small ears, large nostrils, short legs, and enormous arms that can span eight feet. They are of formidable size; a mature male can reach six feet in height and can weigh more than four hundred pounds. The three different gorilla species look very much alike and can easily be confused unless they are placed side by side.

Dian had read of George Schaller's experiences with the gorillas (Schaller 1989) from 1959 through 1960 and wanted to take up the study of the animals where he had left off. Her textbook recommended sitting and observing the gorillas, but she was not satisfied with this approach and decided to elicit their confidence and curiosity by actually acting like a gorilla.

Dian's early years of study were based on trial and error. The Rwandan gorillas had been harassed by poachers and cattle grazers and so rejected her initial attempts to make contact. She imitated their vocalizations when she was sure of what they meant. Once, Dian belched deeply, making the belly rumble of a gorilla who was eating happily, and the gorillas accepted her. She called these sounds *pleasure belches*. Sharp barks in a harsh staccato (pig grunts) meant *behave* and were used in disciplinary situations. A whoop signaled alarm or curiosity. Dian imitated the gorillas' feeding and grooming. Although all this behavior was undignified by human standards, it proved to be rewarding. It enabled her to study the gorillas up close. Dian knew that to save the threatened species, all aspects of the gorillas' behavior had to be thoroughly studied—their diet, mating and reproductive processes, range patterns, and social behavior.

She mapped the gorilla range and began to take a census. In 1970 only 375 mountain gorillas were left in Rwanda, Uganda, and Zaire. Dian found the gorillas to be shy and gentle ground dwellers. The younger ones might nap in trees, but most slept on the ground in nests of foliage, branches, and moss.

Dian learned many things about relating to gorillas: Touching a gorilla is a sign of aggression, so you must instead allow them to touch you. Hum to let them know when you are approaching. Never move suddenly. Never breathe on a gorilla or visit a group of gorillas if you are sick. (Pneumonia is the greatest natural threat to gorillas.) Never run from a gorilla that appears threatening. Gorillas are usually bluffing. Just lumber away and focus your eyes on the ground, and the gorilla will leave you alone. And always give gorillas the right of way.

Initially, Dian observed nine separate gorilla groups, consisting of five to nineteen members in each group, and made close contact with four groups. She numbered the groups and named individual gorillas. They were named and identified by their noses, body structures, shades of fur, and special characteristics or just out of whimsy. Digit was so called because he had a twisted finger. He became Dian's favorite. Beethoven made unusual sounds. Uncle Bert was named after Dian's uncle. Others had such names as Rafiki, Icarus, Peanuts, Geezer, Koko, Samson, Pugnacious, and Whinny.

Each group was led by a dominant silverback (a mature male gorilla, so named because the hair on a gorilla's back turns silver with age), followed in rank by subordinate silverbacks, younger mature males (blackbacks), females, juveniles, and finally infants. Dian observed that gorillas make their own paths. The silverback moves at a steady pace, followed by females and offspring. The immature males circle the group, serving as sentries and guards.

Dian observed that in order to maintain a group's longevity, a strong silverback was needed, with support from a maturing male and enough females for breeding. Dian made a startling discovery. If the gorilla leader died, a power play ensued, and the offspring of the leader were killed. By killing another male's progeny in order to breed with the victims' mother, a male instinctively sought to perpetuate his own lineage. Despite this tragic behavior, more than two thousand hours of Dian's direct observation yielded less than five minutes of true aggression. Most menacing behavior was actually a bluff or a protective action.

A female gorilla reaches maturity at seven years, a male at eight years. Gorillas eat sixty pounds of food a day. Their diet includes snails, slugs, insects, and such vegetation as blackberry leaves, wild celery, thistles, nestles, and galium vines. Their favorite food, the fruit of the *Pygeum africanum* tree, is a delicacy to gorillas.

Much of the gorillas' time is spent at play. In one popular game, a youngster slides down the mother gorilla's body, then eventually down dirt banks and tree trunks. Adults also slide down lava slopes. The adult males are very protective and tolerant of the young, especially during play time.

In 1970 it became necessary for Dian to leave for Cambridge, England, to begin work on her doctoral thesis so that her research could gain validity and acceptance in the scientific community. Right before her departure, during a farewell visit with a gorilla group, the gorilla Peanuts touched her hand. This was the first time a wild gorilla had ever come so close to "holding hands" with a human being. The event was captured in a photograph by Robert Campbell, who spent four years on and off at Karisoke on assignment for *National Geographic* magazine. (During his stay, he and Dian had an ill-fated love affair. When Robert decided to return home, Dian was devastated. Only her commitment to her work kept her going. Dian's friends believe that much of her obsessive behavior in later years was directly related to Robert's rejection of her.)

When Dian returned to Rwanda, her life became increasingly difficult. In 1972 the first research assistant arrived to work with Dian. Others followed, but since the camp was small, space was limited, accommodating only one or two researchers a year. Sometimes much needed funds did not arrive, yet the student assistants and trackers had to be paid. Dian frequently had no substantial food, and she needed dental work. Her health deteriorated. She suffered from emphysema, sciatica, calcium deficiency, insomnia, and a painful limp from a broken leg that had not healed properly. Dian's persistence in tramping through the rain forests and her patience and tenderness toward the animals she cared for resulted in extraordinary discoveries about gorilla behavior. But scientific investigation was not easy.

Dian faced more difficult times, and her life became fraught with danger and hardship. Patrolling the national park area became more trying because of the daily intrusion of Watusi herders, whose cattle destroyed the vegetation the gorillas depended on. The honey gatherers living near the forest were poachers who destroyed the gorillas' habitat by cutting trees that harbored bees' nests. The pygmoid tribe (Batwa) set snares to catch duiker (red forest antelope), and the sounds of the hunt terrified the gorillas. Some got caught in the snares. Woodcutters destroyed the trees. Hunters used the gorillas' body parts to make magical potions. A great deal of money could be made from the skin and bones of gorillas. Gorillas were known as *ngyulla* by the villagers and farmers, and many mystical powers were attributed to them.

Baby gorillas were captured by park guards and tribesmen for European zoos, even though national conservation authorities had declared the gorilla a rare species. Dian fought for the right of the gorillas to remain in their native rain forests, where they belonged. She made many enemies among poachers, cattle herders, park officials, Western conservationists, staff members, and researchers.

Her admiration for the gorillas became her passion. She became more comfortable with them than with humans. They were vulnerable, like her, and only her gorillas remained loyal to her. Dian once said, "I have no friends. The more you learn about the dignity of the gorilla, the more you want to avoid people." Her pet monkey, Kima, and her dog, Cindy, were her friends in camp.

Encroachments on the gorillas' habitat increased. Dian's beloved Digit was slaughtered on 31 December 1977 and was buried in the gorilla graveyard she maintained. She watched her gorilla friends continue to be slaughtered and knew it was done in retaliation against her.

Eventually, getting rid of poachers and keeping human encroachments to a minimum became more important to Dian than science. According to some sources, she resorted to whipping, interrogating, and shooting at her enemies—kidnapping their children, killing their cattle, burning their property, and sending them to jail for their illegal poaching activities. The most notorious poacher, Sebahutu, had received a five-year prison term for poaching, and Dian believed he had a vendetta against her.

In 1979 Dian was at odds with the Mountain Gorilla Project group that wanted to preserve the gorillas by encouraging tourism. Great animosity had also developed between Dian and Laurent Habiyaremije, the director of tourism, who guided dignitaries and tourists into the Karisoke Centre, mainly when Dian was away. Dian became hysterical about tourists' trampling the lush green grass, disturbing the gorillas, and leaving their trash behind. Great pressure was put on Dian to leave Africa.

Habiyaremije forced Dian to make a trek down the mountain into the city every other month to renew her park permit and visa. Because of her emphysema, she spit up blood each time she made the journey back up the mountain. She was in constant pain. But Dian continued to drive herself for the sake of her gorillas. She claimed that she no longer would do research—her assistants could do that under her direction. Her only objective was "to protect these animals."

Funds became more scarce, and Dian could not pay her trackers or assistants. Her behavior became unpopular with those in positions to help her. Some critics say she was an alcoholic, subject to violent mood swings and a bad temper, but Dian drank only when depressed or in physical distress. In 1980, when Dian could no longer manage financially, she left Rwanda for three years to lecture and teach at Cornell University in Ithaca, New York. She also finished her book, *Gorillas in the Mist;* its success made it possible for her to return to Rwanda.

Wayne McGuire arrived at Karisoke on 1 August 1985 as a guest research assistant working on his Ph.D. He was interested in whether silverbacks contribute to infant care and if so, whether this behavior benefits the infant's survival. Wayne saw little of Dian. She spent most of her time in her cabin, where the trackers and assistants gathered each morning for their instructions. She distributed equipment—altimeters, questionnaires, pencils, rain gear, and so forth—then returned to her hut where voluminous correspondence awaited her. She was no longer physically able to track the gorillas.

Her colleagues, who were less dedicated to gorilla protection than she, became increasingly unfriendly. Dian was still opposed to the Mountain Gorilla Project. She was granted only two-month visas and lived in constant fear that they would not be renewed. She continued to lose her closest animal friends and was betrayed by some individuals at Karisoke and by ambitious organizations in Rwanda and abroad.

In 1985 the park conservator issued Dian an invitation to the celebration of the sixtieth anniversary of the Parc National des Volcans after Habiyaremije refused to invite her. (Karisoke is located inside the Parc National.) Awards were given, but Dian was not mentioned, although her work had been made famous in *National Geographic* and had put Rwanda on the map. Habiyaremije's slight of her at this event did not go unnoticed and was widely publicized. This made him despise her even more. Right after Thanksgiving, Dian received a two-year visa to stay in the country, and the immigration service demanded that Habiyaremije give Dian a six-month permit to stay in Karisoke. Dian was elated, but this extension may have been her death sentence.

Dian was far removed from police protection and was easy prey. But she was no fool. Since her arrival in Africa in 1967, she had fully understood the risks to her life.

Dian Fossey's body was found on the floor of her ransacked cabin. A fractured skull and loss of blood were the cause of her death; it was not instantaneous. Police botched the investigation by touching the panga used to kill her. Dian's right hand clutched a clump of hair. Since her doors were locked, the killer apparently entered the cabin by cutting through the corrugated-metal outer wall of her bedroom. No one checked for drugs or poisons to determine whether she had slept through the racket or whether she simply had not been quick enough to escape.

The Rwandan government issued an arrest warrant for Wayne McGuire. He fled to the United States, which has no extradition treaty with Rwanda. In 1987 he was convicted in absentia by the Rwandan government and was sentenced to death by a firing squad. Five Rwandans were charged as accomplices. McGuire still contends that he is innocent, but his academic life is in ruins. The alleged motives were theft of scientific research and professional and personal jealousy. Most people who are familiar with Dian's work say the charge is nonsense, since McGuire already had access to the research data and he did not know enough French and Swahili to enable him to converse with the so-called coconspirators to plan Dian's murder. The mystery of who killed Dian Fossey remains.

Dian was buried beside Digit in the gorilla graveyard among those she loved most. Engraved on her tombstone are these words:

NYIRMACHABELLI
Dian Fossey
1932–1985
No one loved gorillas more
Rest in peace, dear friend
Eternally protected
In this sacred ground
For you are home
Where you belong

At the simple funeral service, the Reverend Elton Wallace offered the following eulogy (Hayes 1990, p. 37):

> Dian Fossey, born to a home of comfort and privilege, she left by her choice to live among a race facing extinction. It was not an easy life, nor would she be widely praised. How often she may have been tempted to give it up and return to her own. But she deemed it worth the sacrifice. And when evil men conspired to take her life she has come to be buried with those among whom she has lived and among whom she has died…. And if you think the distance that Christ came to take the likeness of man is not so great as that from man to gorilla, then you don't know men, or gorillas, or God.

Dian Fossey is known for her studies of the mountain gorilla and for her eighteen-year struggle to save them. They were her family, her love, and her life. She lived and died to protect them. Although her critics may say that her dedication got in the way of common sense, Dian, Nyira-maribi, personified the Rwandan proverb "You can outdistance that which is running after you but not what is running inside you." Dian was in love with life—all of life. She did what great lovers must always do—give themselves completely to those they love.

By 1987 visitors to Karisoke accounted for 60 percent of the country's annual income from tourism. Two hundred forty gorillas survive on the volcanoes of Rwanda and Zaire; 100 more are found in the Bwindi forest of Uganda. The gorilla population has stabilized.

Nancylee (R-J) Richmond-Jeffers
Boone Grove Junior-Senior High School
Boone Grove, Indiana

Suggested Reading

Crouse, Debbie, and Michael Nichols. "Up Close with Gorillas." *International Wildlife* 18 (November–December 1988): 4–11.

Fossey, Dian. *Gorillas in the Mist.* Boston: Houghton Mifflin Co., 1983.

———. "The Imperiled Mountain Gorilla." *National Geographic*, April 1981, pp. 501–23.

Goodall, Alan. *The Wandering Gorillas.* London: William Collins Sons, 1979.

Hayes, Harold T. P. *The Dark Romance of Dian Fossey.* New York: Simon & Schuster, 1990.

———. *The Last Place on Earth.* New York: Stein & Day Publishers, 1983.

Kevles, Bettyann. *Thinking Gorillas: Testing and Teaching the Greatest Apes.* New York: E. P. Dutton, 1980.

Mowat, Farley. *Woman in the Mists: The Story of Dian Fossey and the Mountain Gorillas of Africa.* New York: Warner Books, 1987.

Schaller, George B. *Gorilla: Struggle for Survival in the Virungas.* New York: Aperture, 1989.

Bibliography

Baumgartel, Walter. *Among the Mountain Gorillas.* New York: Harcourt Brace Jovanovich, 1975.

Brower, Montgomery. "The Strange Death of Dian Fossey." *People Weekly*, 17 February 1986, pp. 46–54.

Carr, Rosamond. "Lonely Struggle of the Gorilla Lady." *International Wildlife* 18 (November–December 1988): 12–13.

Fossey, Dian. "Making Friends with Mountain Gorillas." *National Geographic*, January 1970, pp. 48–67.

———. "More Years with Mountain Gorillas." *National Geographic*, October 1971, pp. 574–85.

Hayes, Harold T. P. "Animal Kingdom … or Animal Farm?" *Life*, November 1986, pp. 64–70.

McBee, Susanna. "Great Apes Get New Lease on Life." *U.S. News and World Report*, 9 June 1986, p. 74.

McGuire, Wayne. "I Didn't Kill Dian. She Was My Friend." *Discover*, February 1987, pp. 28–48.

Schaller, George B. *The Year of the Gorilla.* Chicago: University of Chicago Press, 1964.

Veit, Peter. "Case of the Gorilla Lady Murder." *Time*, 1 September 1986, p. 35.

Jane Goodall

—Living among Chimpanzees in Africa

21

When Jane Goodall opened the present for her first birthday, she found a stuffed toy chimpanzee. It was soft and fuzzy. Her family named it Jubilee after the first chimpanzee born in the London Zoo.

The neighbors predicted that a young girl would get nightmares from owning such a toy, but Jane loved Jubilee and even took the stuffed chimp to bed with her. Little did she or her parents know when she was celebrating her first birthday on 3 April 1935 that she would someday live side by side with real chimpanzees.

For most of her childhood and adolescence, Jane lived with her parents. Her father was an engineer, her mother, Vanne, was a homemaker and writer. Her family also included her younger sister, Judy, and two aunts. They lived in a large old brick house called the Birches in Bournemouth, an English seacoast town.

As Jane was growing up, she always loved animals and nature. When Jane was only two, her mother discovered, much to her dismay, that

Jane was sleeping with earthworms under her pillow. And once, when Jane was four, her parents called the police because she had been missing for five hours and they could not find her. Later they learned that she had been sitting in a chicken house, waiting for a hen to lay an egg. "I had always wondered where on a hen was an opening big enough for an egg to come out," Jane recalled. That day she learned for herself.

By the time Jane was seven she had read the *Story of Dr. Doolittle* seven times, as well as the *Jungle Book* and the Tarzan series. When she was eight she had firmly decided that she would someday go to Africa to study wild animals.

Throughout her childhood and her teenage years, Jane did not waver from her lifelong dream of studying wild animals in Africa. Her high school counselor responded, "No girl can do that!" But Jane's mother had taught her never to take no for an answer.

While still a teenager, Jane was hiding in a tree when she overheard her uncle telling her mother that Jane did not have the stamina to study animals in Africa. Rather than weaken her resolve, this incident made Jane even more determined. But while still in high school, Jane suffered a setback. Her hopes of going to college to study science were dashed. After Jane's parents divorced, they did not have enough money to send her to college. So after she finished high school, Jane took a job as a secretary. Nevertheless, she was determined to travel to Africa someday. Several months after Jane took the secretarial position, she received an invitation to visit a friend living in Kenya in Africa. Jane jumped at the chance to go. After saving enough money for the airplane trip, she left for Africa.

While in Africa, Jane stayed for a month with her friend on a farm in Kenya. She still wanted a career working with animals. During this time she heard about Dr. Louis Leakey, a famous scientist who was head of the National Museum of Natural History in Nairobi, the capital of Kenya. Jane went to meet him.

After Jane met Dr. Leakey, he offered her a job in his office. Later he and his wife, Mary, invited Jane to accompany them on one of his paleontological expeditions in Africa. During this trip they taught Jane how to look for bones and tools that might have been used by prehistoric humans.

Jane enjoyed the expedition and the stories that Dr. Leakey told. One day he told her about a group of chimpanzees living near Lake Tanganyika in Tanzania. Dr. Leakey wanted someone to study the chimps—someone who had not been preconditioned and taught by other scientists. He was looking for a person who would observe the animals in their natural habitat and record the observations daily. Jane wanted a chance to study the chimpanzees.

Dr. Leakey needed time to secure financing for the project. Jane waited patiently while all the arrangements were planned. By 1960, when Jane was twenty-six, financing for a six-month study was arranged with the Wilkie Foundation.

The local government, however, would not allow a woman, especially an English woman, to live alone in the jungle. To study the chimpanzees, Jane had to take a group of people with her. She convinced her mother to go with her, along with an African cook, Dominic, and a few African men who would row the boat and set up camp. On arriving at Gombe Stream in Tanzania, they decided to camp in a flat, peaceful location near the stream.

They set up their tents, and Dominic cooked their meals over an open campfire. Life was simple. Jane wore her hair in a ponytail to prevent it from becoming tangled in the thorns and brush as she ventured into the forest. At times she was so engrossed in her work that she did not even return to camp for meals. She simply ate beans from a can while she observed the chimpanzees from her vantage point.

For the first few days Jane did not see any chimps. She kept returning to the area where she thought they would be. Then one day she heard them, and by using a set of binoculars that she always carried with her, she could also see them. She was unable to get close to the chimps at first because as soon as they heard her coming through the jungle, they would leave the area. It was difficult to view them through the binoculars in this area because the forest was very thick. Day after day, Jane walked through the undergrowth. She finally realized that when she sat very still, the chimps did not run away. After weeks of watching, Jane began giving names to the chimps. To one large male who had a gray beard around his chin, Jane gave the name David Greybeard. The old female with tattered ears and a big, bulbous nose became Flo. And Ollie got her name because her coat reminded Jane of her aunt Olwen's hairstyle.

One day during the first year of her observations, as Jane was sitting on a high perch in the forest, she saw a small group of three chimps—a male, a female, and a youngster—in a tree below her. Jane recognized the male chimp. It was David Greybeard. Jane observed that David would take a bite of some pink matter, pick some leaves from the tree, and then chew it all together. Occasionally he would take a small piece of the pink substance and place it in the female's outstretched hand; then she would eat it. David dropped a piece, and the youngster scrambled to the ground below to pick it up and eat it. At the time Jane did not know for certain what they were eating. After the chimps left, Jane searched the area and discovered that they had been eating a small piglet. Scientists had thought that chimps ate only fruits, vegetation, and, occasionally, insects and small rodents. Jane had learned something new about their behavior. This discovery was exciting.

As Jane followed the chimps through the forest day after day, carefully recording the behavior and habits she observed, she had to be careful not to get too close. She learned that the chimps became easily excited. When they were excited, they picked up rocks and threw them or picked up tree branches and waved them around. A male chimp is about four feet tall, weighs nearly one hundred pounds, and is more than twice as strong as a full-grown man. If Jane had got too close before the chimps had learned to trust her, she might have been seriously injured.

Twice that year Jane made startling discoveries. Her second observation occurred when she had been tramping through the dense undergrowth of the forest for hours and had not seen a single chimp. Suddenly she stopped. She had noticed a slight movement in the tall grass about sixty yards away. Through her binoculars she saw David Greybeard poking into a hole in the ground with a blade of grass, then bringing the blade of grass up to his mouth. Quietly, she moved to a better position from which to watch. She saw David squatting beside the red-dirt mound of a termite nest.

Jane watched for more than an hour. When David had eaten his fill of termites, he left the area. Jane went to the termite nest and tried using a blade of grass in the same way she had seen David use it. She poked a blade of grass into the termite mound and waited. In a few seconds she felt a tug on the grass. When she pulled the grass out of the hole, she found several termites clinging to the grass with their teeth and frantically kicking their legs in midair. David had been fishing for termites with a blade of grass as his fishing pole.

Jane had heard about two other occasions on which observers had recorded chimpanzees' using tools to obtain food. Once a chimp had used a rock as a hammer to break open a palm nut, and another time a group of chimps had been seen pushing sticks into an underground bees' nest and then licking the honey off the sticks. Jane had never expected to observe such exciting behavior herself.

Jane learned many things about chimpanzees, for instance, that they hold hands and even kiss one another. Jane wrote down what she saw and learned because she knew Dr. Leakey would want to know all the facts.

She realized that she was observing some significant scientific discoveries firsthand. But without the scientific knowledge that college affords, Jane realized that she could not become a spokesperson for the scientific community. With Dr. Leakey's help, Jane received college credit for her in-field observations and was admitted to a Ph.D. program at Cambridge University in England in 1961. For the next several years, she spent a few months each winter studying at Cambridge and the rest of the year in Africa. She earned a doctorate in ethology (the study of animal behavior) in 1965.

As time passed, others heard about the woman who was living among the chimpanzees in Africa. The National Geographic Society became interested in Jane's studies of the chimps and then began to finance her work. Later the society hired Hugo van Lawick to photograph the chimps. After Hugo arrived in Jane's camp in 1962, he visually documented what Jane had been seeing and recording on paper.

Born in Indonesia, Hugo was a Dutch baron who had been working as a photographer and filmmaker in East Africa. He and Jane had much in common: both felt a keen interest in the animal world and were dedicated to their careers. Together they were able to accomplish much more than either one of them could have accomplished alone.

The chimps began trusting Jane and Hugo and allowed them to come closer and closer. Sometimes while Jane and Hugo were observing them, the chimps would even pull at Hugo's camera or pluck at his or Jane's shirt.

Hugo and Jane became friends as well as coworkers. After they had worked together for more than a year, Hugo asked Jane to marry him. She was visiting family members in England when she received his cable that read, "Will you marry me stop love stop Hugo." Jane immediately accepted his proposal, and they were married on 28 March 1964 in London.

Instead of the usual statue of a bride and groom, their wedding cake was topped with a clay chimpanzee. The walls of the reception hall were decorated with large color photographs that Hugo had taken of the chimpanzees.

Three weeks before the wedding, Jane had received word from Dominic, her camp's cook, that Flo had given birth. The newlyweds cut their honeymoon short and rushed back to Gombe to see and photograph Flo's new baby.

For the next three years, Jane and Hugo watched and recorded the behavior of the chimps at Gombe reserve. They observed that Flo was a calm and tolerant mother. When her young four-year-old daughter, Fifi, tried to touch the new baby, Flint, Flo pushed her hand gently aside. Time and again Jane and Hugo watched as Flo reacted gently and reassuringly to her young son and daughter. She would often distract Fifi and Flint by tickling them when they were attracted to some mischief.

Jane labeled Flo the model mother, and both she and Hugo decided that Flo's methods would be good parenting techniques for humans as well. They resolved to practice this behavior when they had a child of their own.

In 1967 they got that opportunity; Hugo and Jane had a son. They named him Hugo Eric Louis, but his nickname, Grub, which means bush baby, was the name that stuck as he grew up in Africa. Jane and Hugo believed that a child should remain in close contact with his or her parents, so they took Grub with them as they explored Gombe's streams, forests, and beaches.

Although their friends were concerned about Jane and Hugo's raising their son in the wilds of Africa, Grub, now an adult, is a well-spoken, courteous, handsome, and adventurous young man. During his years at Gombe, he became an expert swimmer, fisher, and explorer.

Jane still pulls her now-graying hair into a ponytail. But she is no longer the awestruck young woman she was in 1960; she has become a world-renowned scientist. Jane has survived great tragedy over the years: divorce from Hugo when Grub was seven and the death of her second husband from cancer in 1980. Most of the chimps she knew when she first went to Gombe have died. Flo's daughter, Fifi, is still living and has a large family of her own. Jane enjoys spending time with them when she is in Africa.

Jane continues to carry on the work she began with the chimpanzees in 1960. Since then, she has written many books about them. Some of these books have photographs of David Greybeard, Flo, and Ollie, along with pictures of Jane, Hugo, and Grub.

In addition to writing books, Jane has visited many countries to teach others what she has learned. She has established a research center at

Gombe Stream, where college students can study and do research. She has also established the Goodall Institute in Tucson, Arizona.

Jane now divides her time each year, spending six months in Africa and six months giving lectures throughout the world and sharing her vast knowledge of the chimpanzees of Africa.

Marilyn Thompson Drang
Lincoln Junior High School
Plymouth, Indiana

Suggested Reading

Fox, Mary Virginia. *Jane Goodall, Living Chimp Style.* Minneapolis, Minn.: Dillon Press, 1981.

Goodall, Jane. *Through a Window: My Thirty Years with the Chimpanzees of Gombe.* Boston: Houghton Mifflin Co., 1990.

Montgomery, Sy. *Walking with the Great Apes.* Boston: Houghton Mifflin Co., 1990.

van Lawick, Jane Goodall. *In the Shadow of Man.* Boston: Houghton Mifflin Co., 1971.

van Lawick, Jane Goodall, and Hugo van Lawick. *Innocent Killers.* Boston: Houghton Mifflin Co., 1971.

Mary Gray

—Advocate for Women in Mathematics

On 4 October 1957—a beautiful fall day in most of the United States—a startling new sound is heard by military and civilian tracking stations around the world. "Beep, beep … beep, beep." The Union of Soviet Socialist Republics has caught the world, especially the United States, by surprise! The first artificial satellite, *Sputnik I*, has just been launched. The race for space has begun.

In homes, offices, stores, and schools around the country, everyone expresses shock and dismay that the Soviets have been the first to get a satellite into space. Concern deepens when on 3 November *Sputnik II*, larger and carrying the dog Laika, is launched into orbit. Many Americans fear for the first time that since the Soviets are the first into space, they must also be scientifically and technically superior.

High-level officials try to play down the momentous event; nevertheless, the citizenry is alarmed. Such questions as, How did we let this happen? and What can we do to catch up? are heard everywhere. People begin to question whether the scientific and mathematical training that young people receive in school is adequate. They wonder if more people need to study mathematics and science in order for the United States to regain the technical lead. The government's response is to increase its commitment to the sciences by giving many more grants and scholarships to high school and college students who intend to enter these fields.

At Hastings College in Nebraska, the news that the government would financially support students studying mathematics and science helps one young student make up her mind about which career to pursue. Although equally interested in law, Mary Wheat Gray chooses mathematics.

Born in Kansas on 8 April 1939, Mary was the only child in a family that supported her decision to study whatever she wished. Like her peers, she did chores around the house and went to football games. Mary never chose activities simply because they were thought to be suitable for either girls or boys; she got involved in pursuits because they interested her. She liked school. Her favorite subjects were mathematics, history, and physics. Her mother hoped that Mary would someday become a high school mathematics teacher. Teaching was a very common profession for a woman in those days. But Mary had something different in mind. In time, Mary would astound everyone she knew with her achievements.

Mary's father died while she was still in high school, so no money was available for college. But because she did so well academically, Mary earned a full scholarship to Hastings College and graduated from there in 1959 at the top of her class.

On graduation from Hastings, Mary received a prestigious Fulbright scholarship. Fulbright scholarships, begun in 1946, are government scholarships sponsored by the United States Department of State to promote mutual understanding and educational exchanges between the United States and other countries. Qualified applicants must have a college degree and a knowledge of the language of the country in which they wish to study. The full scholarship covers the cost of transportation, books, tuition, and living expenses for one academic year. Mary used her scholarship to study mathematics at Johann Wolfgang von Goethe Universität in Frankfurt, Germany, in 1959 and 1960.

Returning to the United States, she quickly earned her master's degree in 1962 and her doctorate in mathematics in 1964. Both her graduate degrees were from the University of Kansas. Professor James Standley, the chair of the Department of Mathematics, was both helpful and encouraging. He could see that Mary possessed great talent and abilities in mathematics. Mary was the first woman since 1926 to earn a Ph.D. in mathematics from the University of Kansas!

In the 1950s, being a girl and studying mathematics was not easy. Very few young women studied advanced mathematics. In high school, girls were given the subtle social message that girls do not normally study mathematics. Very few girls took four years of mathematics in high school. Only two or three young women might be enrolled in advanced mathematics at a college. Only 5 percent of the students graduating in the 1950s with doctorates in mathematics were women. Given such an atmosphere, Mary's achievements are even more notable.

Graduating from college with an advanced degree in mathematics does not guarantee suitable employment. In the 1960s it was not too difficult for a female mathematician to find a job as a teacher in a high school (remember that this is what Mary's mother had wanted her to do) or as an untenured mathematics instructor in a college. But it was almost unheard of for a woman to be a full professor of mathematics or to be a research mathematician.

After receiving her doctorate in mathematics in 1964, Mary quickly moved through the academic ranks. She was a mathematics instructor at the University of California at Berkeley and then became an assistant professor, and later an associate professor, at California State University at Hayward. During this time Mary was married to Alfred Gray, also a mathematician. In 1968 American University in Washington, D.C., appointed Mary an associate professor; she was promoted to full professor in 1971 in the Department of Mathematics, Statistics, and Computer Science. She has remained there ever since.

About the time that Mary became a full professor, she attended an annual meeting of the American Mathematical Society (AMS) in Atlantic

City, New Jersey. She was one of a group of women at the meeting who formed a women's caucus to discuss women's status in mathematics. (A caucus is a meeting of a small group of people to discuss a policy.) Mary also staged a one-person sit-in at the meeting of the AMS ruling inner council, which consisted only of men. (A sit-in is a nonviolent protest demonstration.) When asked to leave, Mary refused, saying that the AMS had no rules that restricted attendance at the meeting. When she was told that the meeting was restricted by "gentlemen's agreement," she replied, "Well, obviously I'm no gentleman!" After Mary's protest, the council meetings were open to observers, and the society became much more democratic.

In February 1971, Mary placed a small announcement in the *Notices of the American Mathematical Society* about a new organization that was being formed for female mathematicians. This group became the Association for Women in Mathematics (AWM), and Mary was elected its first president. Her goals for the group included exposing discrimination against female mathematicians, providing support and information to fellow women in mathematics, and spreading the word that girls "can and should" learn mathematics. All during the 1970s, Mary and others in the AWM worked to increase people's awareness of women in mathematics and thus improve their image.

You may remember that in 1959, the reason Mary chose to study mathematics rather than law in graduate school was that financial aid was available from the government to do so. In the late 1970s Mary realized a long-awaited goal. She received her law degree from American University, was admitted to the bar in the District of Columbia, and became eligible to argue before the United States Supreme Court. She was pleased that she would be able to use her knowledge of law and statistics to investigate and prove cases of discrimination against women and minorities in the workplace.

From the 1970s until the present, Mary has been active in many organizations. Among them are Amnesty International, the American Association of University Professors, the American Mathematical Society, and the

Association for Women in Mathematics. In addition, she is a member of mathematical societies in England and France. Mary has also been chair of her department at American University several times.

During Mary's professional career, she has taken aim at many social injustices. Mary has used her precisely honed skills in the areas of mathematics, statistics, law, and computer science to respond to human needs. Beginning in the 1970s, Mary became zealously involved in trying to improve the opportunities and status of women in mathematics and in the academic world in general. As a highly visible public speaker and writer about these subjects, Mary has called attention to discrimination and inequities involving women and minorities in the areas of mathematics education, academic freedom, university employment, insurance and pension benefits, and academic tenure.

After Mary received her law degree, her interests expanded to include statistics and the use of statistics in legal proceedings—forensic statistics. Much of her current research is in this area and in the new area of computer law. An interesting example of a recent problem in computer law is the following question: If a business has all its records stored in a computer system and the system fails, thereby losing all the information, can the manufacturer of the computer be sued? With her knowledge of computers, statistics, and the law, Mary would be an expert witness in a case of this type.

Mary is highly respected for her achievements. She travels worldwide to speak out against violations of human rights. At American University, Mary encourages women and minorities to pursue careers in mathematics. One-fourth of the faculty members in her department are women, and the majority of Mary's doctoral students are also women. Although Mary has no children of her own, she has been a role model for many young women. Her influence is likely to increase every year.

The status of women in mathematics has certainly changed since the 1950s. In the United States today, more than 20 percent of the people earning doctorates in mathematics each year are women. Now when someone says the word *mathematician,* we do not always think "he." For this, we have people like Mary Gray to thank. She is an ideal role model. She proves that women can be successful in mathematics and can reach the highest levels of achievement, even in more than one field. Such success requires perseverance, drive, energy, and most important, a love for mathematics.

Carolyn Evans Moreland
Elkhart Central High School
Elkhart, Indiana

Suggested Reading

Blum, Lenore. "A Brief History of the Association for Women in Mathematics: The Presidents' Perspective." *Notices of the American Mathematical Society* 38 (September 1991): 738–54.

Jackson, Allyn. "Top Producers of Women Mathematics Doctorates." *Notices of the American Mathematical Society* 38 (September 1991): 715–19.

Kenschaft, Patricia C., ed. *Winning Women into Mathematics*. Washington, D.C.: Mathematical Association of America, 1991.

Morgenstern, Ellen. "Profile: Mary Gray." *Academe* (September 1979): 368–69.

Mozans, H. J. *Woman in Science*. Notre Dame, Ind.: University of Notre Dame Press, 1991.

Illustrations by

KEVIN C. CHADWICK

Mr. Chadwick is a nationally known illustrator in the art of scratchboard. His ability to render light, depth, and expression in this traditional medium brings his subjects to life.

He lives and works with his wife, Suzanne, a graphic designer, in their two-century-old home in the historic village of Waterford, Virginia.

Printed by

STEPHENSON PRINTING
Alexandria, Virginia

Typography

Typeset in Caslon, Isadora, and Tiepolo

Paper by

MOHAWK PAPER MILLS

The cover is printed on Splendorlux. The text is printed on Mohawk Opaque.